# A Wanderer's Guide to New Mexico

## A Collection of Trips and Excursions Through the Land of Enchantment

### Volume I
### SALLY INTO THE SOUTHWEST QUADRANT

SOCORRO
MAGDALENA
KELLY
RILEY
TRUTH OR CONSEQUENCES
HILLSBORO
DEMING
COLUMBUS
PALOMAS
HACHITA
ANTELOPE WELLS
And Places in Between . . . .

by K. HILLESON

Photography by D. Nakii

Graphics by Betty Jo Colvin
Copyright 1985 by D. Nakii Enterprises
Produced and Published by D. Nakii Enterprises
P.O. Box 7639, Albuquerque, New Mexico 87194

This book is dedicated to
my friend
GEORGE HANKINS
A famous New Mexican wanderer
whom the world never
properly recognized.

ISBN 0-9615195-0-9

# TABLE OF CONTENTS

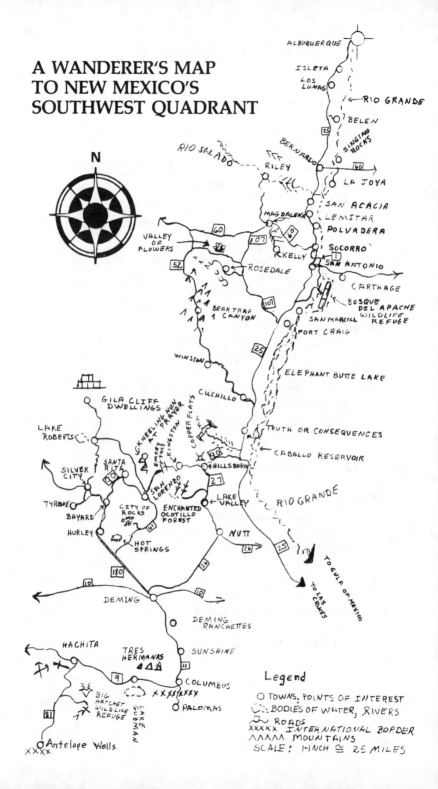

# A WANDERER'S MAP
# TO NEW MEXICO'S
# SOUTHWEST QUADRANT

N

ALBUQUERQUE
ISLETA
LOS LUNAS
← RIO GRANDE
BELEN
25
SINGING ROCKS
RIO SALADO
BERNARDO
60
LA JOYA
RILEY
SAN ACACIA
LEMITAR
MAGDALENA
POLVADERA
VALLEY OF FLOWERS
60
107
6
SOCORRO
52
KELLY
SAN ANTONIO
ROSEDALE
1
CARTHAGE
101
BOSQUE DEL APACHE WILDLIFE REFUGE
BEAR TRAP CANYON
SAN MARCIAL
FORT CRAIG
25
WINSTON
ELEPHANT BUTTE LAKE
CUCHILLO
GILA CLIFF DWELLINGS
KNEELING NUN AT PRAYER
COPPER FLATS
LAKE ROBERTS
EMORY PASS
KINGSTON
TRUTH OR CONSEQUENCES
CABALLO RESERVOIR
SILVER CITY
SANTA RITA
HILLSBORO
TYRONE
SAN LORENZO
27
RIO GRANDE
BAYARD
CITY OF ROCKS
ENCHANTED OCOTILLO FOREST
LAKE VALLEY
HURLEY
61
HOT SPRINGS
NUTT
26
25
TO GULF OF MEXICO
180
24
TO LAS CRUCES
10
DEMING
10
DEMING RANCHETTES
HACHITA
TRES HERMANAS
SUNSHINE
9
11
COLUMBUS
BIG HATCHET WILDLIFE REFUGE
XXXX XXXX
LAKE GUZMAN
PALOMAS
81
Antelope Wells
XXXX

## Legend

○ TOWNS, POINTS OF INTEREST
◌ BODIES OF WATER, RIVERS
∿ ROADS
XXXXX INTERNATIONAL BORDER
∧∧∧∧∧ MOUNTAINS
SCALE: 1-INCH ≅ 25 MILES

# INTRODUCTION: Caveat Emptor

*This is not an accurate guide book. It is not in the same class as Michelin's Guide to Europe or Baedeker's. It is not definitive and it is not conclusive. Rather it is a loving look at a beloved place. It is a tour of home, so it naturally includes all those lies, myths and old skeletons that accumulate around old family estates. It is not objective. I have visited and recorded the people and places that I care about and have left out everything else.*

*There are probably more worthy and maybe more interesting, yea, even more important places to see in the land of New Mexico but they aren't in this book. Maybe those are the places you should find for yourself. Wanderers, after all, do that. They travel slowly and look about. They have vague goals and are ready to see what is on the other side of the hill. They look at the customs and habits of the people and pass on. Among the greatest wanderers were Sacajewa, Marco Polo, Christopher Columbus, Daniel Boone and Ragnar Hairy Breeks (the first Viking to sack Paris). Although these people have been assigned purpose and motive by history, the most outstanding fact about them was that they had the courage to leave home and go wandering about. What they did upon reaching their various turn-around points has nothing to do with us. They went and they looked. And they seemed to have had a good time. A hell of a good time!*

# HOW TO USE THIS BOOK

Put this book in your car. Drive down the highway. When you get bored or see something you wished you knew about, look in the book. It might be there.

When out of state visitors come to visit, we get in the car and go to look at the Land of Enchantment. As we drive along, I tell them all the stories, lies, scientific scraps and historical bits of information about the countryside that is passing by. I recount scandals and adventures that have happened at different places. I tell of personal experiences that may never happen to anyone else or may always happen in a certain location. We do not go to major and important tourist areas and improve out minds. We do not learn as much as we can. We do not travel by the quickest road with an equipment list and a mileage chart. We do enjoy seasonal pleasures. We have time on our hands and a desire to share what it means to live in this state. This is what I have tried to put in this book.

This book will be useless to the traveler like Gary Reese, a sales engineer from the East. When asked if he had ever driven from Farmington to Shiprock, the man replied, "Yes, and it was the Devil's creation! I'm never going back there again!"

If you insist on driving with your eyes closed and your mind shut, you won't like this book. It is for those with the wandering spirit who will drive onto a mesa or into a small and dusty town and start to imagine what life might be like there. It is a conversation between the road, the stopping places, and the heart.

# I

# Albuquerque to Socorro

### Isleta Pueblo

### Belen

### Bernardo

### La Joya

### Rio Salado Rest Stop

### Socorro

### And points in between

# LEAVE ALBUQUERQUE _____

Going south on Interstate 25, the snow-capped Ladrone Mountains are visible in the far distance on your right. Although *"ladrone"* translates into *"thief"* in Spanish and the rough and rocky canyons were known to be a safe hideout for badmen, there are no tales of buried treasure or golden loot here. The loot of the ladrones in this area was mostly four-footed.

As you pass the industrial areas and dead car lots on the Albuquerque outskirts, the highway begins a long, slow curve to the right. You'll know where you are if you can see the Karler Packing Plant or the chicken ranch on your right. Both of them are identifiable by smell. Now, looking into the distance you can see the Magdalena Mountains south or left of the Ladrones and you start twitching with wanderlust. Try to decide whether to take Highway 60 out of Socorro and go on to the old cowtown of Magdalena and the mining ghost towns of Kelly and Riley on the Rio Salado or whether to stick on I-25 and get off by Caballo Lake and take the winding two lane through the Black Range to Hillsboro and Emory Pass. Don't fret, you have about seventy-five miles to make the decision.

Twenty miles out of Albuquerque and approaching Los Lunas, the ribbon of green on your left shows the path of the Rio Grande that has just passed through the Isleta Indian Reservation. The Manzano Mountains are on your left and a new industry for New Mexico, sod ranching, will be on your right. The land sweeps to the horizon flat and sere.

# ISLETA _____

The Isleta Indians are a progressive people. Entire Ph.D. dissertations have been written about them, and you could spend a very pleasant autumn afternoon wandering around their pueblo and looking at their church. They are excellent bread bakers and farmers, and have very skilled potters and jewelers among their members. They are also one of the few people in modern times to stand up to the Catholic Church and defy that powerful and religious body. When the priest assigned to their pueblo was critical and overly dogmatic concerning their practice of the old religion, alongside of the Catholic one, the elders of the pueblo threw the priest out rather than change. This caused quite a stir and the matter was not peaceably settled for several years, during which the pueblo was without an official Catholic representative.

The church is quite interesting in that the bodies of several respected people are buried in the floor of the church near the altar. This is, of course, an old Spanish tradition brought to the New World. In Spain, the wealthy patrons or worthy citizens were interred in the cathedrals instead of in cemeteries. Their bodies were placed in ornate marble crypts and mausoleums in the walls of the churches. In the simpler churches of the New World, they had to settle for burial in the floor. Now it is said that when there is going to be a good harvest for the Iseltans, the old graves shift and move up to the floor of the church to let the people know. It is also said that this happens when there is a particularly wet spring and the water tables rise causing the graves to shift. Fortunately everyone gets to believe what they want.

Take the Los Lunas exit off the highway, turn to your left at the top of the exit ramp and head east one half mile to the pay phone at the gas station on your right. That is mostly a mobile home with pumps. This is the last easily accessible pay phone that is not a long distance call to Albuquerque. Check the stock market or call your office for the last time. Then retrace your path back to the highway and head south.

Looking left you can see the plowed and furrowed fields of the prison farm spread below Tome Hill. This is a minimum security prison for not-too-serious offenders and you might someday hear someone mention something about *"feeding the turkeys down in Los Lunas for a few years."* You will know they are talking about a stretch at the prison farm.

Tome Hill is a real hill, not a small mountain. From the highway you can clearly see the winding path that takes both the hang glider pilots as well as the religious pilgrims to the top where a large white cross stands. Though it appears innocent from the Interstate, Tome Hill has been the scene of several fatal hang glider accidents. An experienced glider pilot of thirty-eight who had seen many flights from Tome and had finally given up the sport, once remarked, "There aren't any OLD hang gliders."

# BELEN

Thirty-two miles from Albuquerque, is little Belen. Although named in 1888 for the old city of Bethlehem , Belen is the new mecca for commuters who want to raise their families in the country. Once the hub of all rail traffic in the Southwest, Belen is now noted mostly for its colorfully painted water tower and for Pete's Cafe, a railway man's heaven. Pete's is located right across the tracks from the railroad station and it serves great Mexican food. It was eventually "discovered" and forced to expand. Although it now has a more gracious decor, it still serves the railway workers some of the best chile in the state.

Every sack of grain, bolt of cloth and farm implement used by the people in the small communities of this area used to be drop-shipped to the railhead at Belen. And travelers to the south and east used to drive out of Albuquerque to catch the train in order to avoid the trouble of boarding in the Duke City and changing trains in Belen. With the demise of the railroad traffic, Belen too, dwindled and grew sleepy

After Belen, the Interstate carries you by small farming and ranching operations. These are part of traditional agriculture in America. These are not Agri-business corporations, but family businesses and a way of life.

About forty-four miles from Albuquerque, the vineyards of the Rio Grande Cellars will show up on your right. Another new idea in New Mexico agriculture, the rows of neatly staked grapevines extend for at least a mile alongside the highway. Just as they end, a tall, square building with gothic doors announces the headquarters of the winery. It takes three years for a grapevine to start producing commercially, and hopes are high that the state will become a strong area for viniculture.

The Interstate is now following the fly-way of the sandhill cranes that winter at the Bosque Del Apache Wildlife Refuge. In late winter and early autumn, great flocks of sandhill cranes will be flying overhead in their annual journeys between New Mexico and Idaho. If you stop your car and get out to listen, you will be able to hear them crying in shrill raucous tones as they fly. You will be able to hear them before you see them. If you are lucky and have keen eyes or binoculars, you might even see a whooping crane flying with them.

The whooper, an endangered species, is making a comeback under a Federally sponsored program that borrows whooping crane eggs from captive female whoopers with extra ones and slips them into sandhill crane nests in the wild. The sandhill cranes then incubate and raise the whoopers. No one knows what sandhill crane mothers think when one of their nestlings grows up to be twice the size of everyone else, but apparently maternal instincts dominate and the whoopers are thriving with the sandhill crane flocks.

# BERNARDO

Bernardo, fifty miles out of Albuquerque is a good place to stop and stretch your legs. Although there is a gas station and a small store there, you can also take the branch highway on your right from the top of the exit ramp, old Highway 285, down to the old iron trestle bridge and stop there for a walk and a stretch. The Bernardo area is known for singing rocks. I do not know how or why the rocks can be made to sing. Check this out for yourself.

# LA JOYA

La Joya is next. *"The Jewel"* as it translates from Spanish, is another small farming community. It is also the site of another game refuge. Some of the farmers in this area are subsidized by the Federal Government to plant grain for the migratory waterfowl and to flood their fields in the winter to provide a safe place for these birds to spend the colder months. The ducks, cranes and geese spend their winter days flying between the Bosque Del Apache and the La Joya fields.

In the summer there is a weekend fiesta at La Joya which I have never attended. Look for posters in the windows of small stores and gas stations around La Joya starting in July. Sooner or later you'll get the time and date. People from La Joya say it's a good time.

## Rio Salado Rest Stop

The next point of interest on I-25 is the Rio Salado *(Salt River)* Rest Stop. These are among the very few state buildings in New Mexico that are not built in the Colonial-Adobe style. The story is that because of the shifting, changing nature of the sand dunes here on the banks of the Rio Salado, it was not feasible to use the traditional state architecture for the rest stop. Instead, the buildings were put on stilts above the sand and were thus made safe. This sounds like bull to me but it's a story I've heard often enough.

The river here trickles, muds, and sometimes floods. It is always sandy, salty, and dusty. The wind blows constantly and it is about as far as you can get from a traditional river.

For those who wish a dose of true, old-fashioned wandering, pack your backpack with water and hike up the river to the old town of Riley. It's about twenty miles, and you will get to experience the real desert-nomad type of wandering. You may meet wetbacks, cowboys, dust storms, cattle, and assorted desert animals. Or equally likely, nobody and nothing. You will probably not meet any drinking water or cool shady oases. Be intelligent about this. This is a strip of land where you can lose your way and lose your life because of the lack of water and the high temperatures. Such a trip is a picnic only if you're prepared and think about what you're doing.

# II

# Socorro to Truth or Consequences
## by way of:
## San Antonio
## Carthage
## The Bosque Del Apache Wildlife Refuge
## Fort Craig
## San Marcial

Halfway between the town of Riley and the highway there is an old house on the side of the river. After hiking the river, I went and looked up the old couple who used to live there. Their life in the desert was beyond ordinary experience and it was well worth listening to them talk. They may still be running the bar Bernardo.

From La Joya to Socorro, the Rio Grande Valley is dotted with small villages with exotic names. San Acacia, named for the early Roman martyr, Sant Acacio, is there. Lemitar is named for a prominent founding family as well as a local and common plant. Polvadera is the dusty spot, but bees do well here.

Before World War II, this was a rich truck farming area. It was not uncommon for the farmers to load a wagon with fresh produce and spend a day traveling to the desert towns of Magdalena, Kelly, or even Datil. Another day would go by as they sold their green stuff to the residents of those towns, and a third day would see the farmer home. The profit for this three day excursion might be twenty or twenty-five dollars, a goodly sum for those times, and of course there was the pleasure of the adventure.

# SOCORRO

Seventy-five miles out of Albuquerque and you begin to see the outskirts of Socorro or *"Help"* in Spanish. Not really as comical as it sounds, it is a shortened form of the Virgin Mary's title, Our Lady of Perpetual Help. Socorro is a town that is home to New Mexico Tech, a university noted for engineers in mining and petroleum, as well as physicists and other technical scientists. It is also the supply point to ranchers, modern day prospectors and tourists passing along the Interstate.

Socorro is a place of decision. From here you may turn west and on to Magdalena. Or you may go straight on to the south, heading for Las Cruces and ultimately, Mexico. Then again, this is the point to get off the Interstate and go visit the ghost town of Carthage or the Bosque Del Apache Wildlife Refuge. While you are deciding, look around Socorro.

On the way into Socorro, before you are offered an exit from the freeway, you can spot a large complex of buildings on the right side of the road. This was originally a cotton mill which was supposed to have revolutionized Socorro's industry. When the dream didn't turn to reality, the realtors began to offer the buildings to anyone who needed commercial space. It has been a wide variety of things, and at my last visit it was a wholesale jewelry concern. At one time or another it seems, almost every business in New Mexico has been involved in the turquoise and silver jewelry trade. It might be endemic, like the dust, Quien sabe?

Once in the city of Socorro, there is much to keep a wanderer entertained. The campus of New Mexico Tech is pleasant to stroll, and the library often has an interesting selection of art on its walls. As you walk you can wonder if you are seeing the next Albert Einstein or the next astronaut going past you. The students at New Mexico Tech take their science very seriously. They also hold one of the few pickleball tournaments in the USA. (Pickleball is similar to paddleball, but not quite.) Like all engineering schools they have a bit of madness on Saint Patrick's Day. (Engineers selected Saint Patrick as their patron saint because he drove the snakes out of Ireland. Engineers think he did this with some type of engineering. The logic of this does not seem to bother the engineers.) Among the most notable flights of fancy that New Mexico Techies have tried, is driving a golfball up or down the slopes of the mountain behind the school. This makes such standard mining contests as pneumatic drilling seem a little staid. The male students at NMT usually outnumber the females and this is a traditional source of grumbling on the campus. Occasionally an enterprising soul has hired a bus and done some advance publicity among the women at the University of New Mexico campus. The bus is supposed to go to Albuquerque, pick up a load of coeds who want a change of scene, and return to Socorro with the ladies for a (free!) romantic weekend in Socorro. I've never talked with anyone who actually participated in this venture, so you can regard it as either a piece of folklore, or a tribute to lust and enterprise.

Within walking distance, south of the campus, is the old center of town. Here, there is a small but pleasant plaza with shade trees and benches. Some of the older residents spend their days here on the benches under the trees. No one will mind if you spend time here, too. In fact, they will enjoy seeing you as much as you enjoy seeing them. A fair exchange. In Socorro, sometimes a man might gently tease his wife by threatening to retire early just so he can go down to the plaza every day.

From the plaza you can see the Capitol Bar. This is an old establishment and is considered the college hangout, but many non-student types also hang out at the Capitol. It has a nice serious ring to it, to say, "I'm going to the Capitol." It's a pleasant, dark spot to drink a beer or two.

Back on the main street of Socorro, as you head south, keep a sharp lookout to your left. You will easily be able to spot a large, handpainted, and old advertisement for White Owl Cigars. It is on the side of the brick building across from the movie theatre. It's a lovely bit of public art, and a craft that is not practiced anymore.

Eating in Socorro is an adventure all by itself. You will be able to pick out the standard drive-ins, coffee shops, and road food restaurants with no trouble. There is a noteable Chinese chef in Socorro who moves from restaurant to restaurant, so if you see an advertisement for this kind of cooking, you might stop and give it a try. If you desire Mexican cuisine, a place called La Casita serves chile that will make your face red and your ears burn. But they do it lovingly. You will be able to find all these places from the main street, so it's pointless trying to give directions for them.

If you have decided to see the Bosque Del Apache, San Antonio, and the ruins of Carthage, you must take the *"old road"* out of Socorro. It is now called Highway 285, but just look for the sign that says San Antonio or the Bosque Del Apache Wildlife Refuge. Basically, this is a left turn off the main drag.

Eleven miles south of Socorro, you will see San Antonio. It is named for Saint Anthony of Padua, who was a student of Saint Francis of Assisi. Although San Antonio appears to be a modest little village, it is noteworthy to the world because it is the birthplace of Conrad Hilton, the great hotel magnate. There is not a Hilton Hotel here now, but Conrad was born in a boarding house run by his parents and apparently that is where he got the start for his guest house empire. The world is probably a more civilized place because of Conrad Hilton. When he was just launching his business, he offered partnerships to several Albuquerque businessmen; they all turned him down. He went it alone.

San Antonio's current claim to fame is the Owl Cafe. Many people say that the very best hamburgers in the USA come out of the kitchen at the Owl Bar and Cafe. The Owl's owners have frozen and shipped their American specialty to hungry patrons all over the map, and the scientists at White Sands Missile Range have brought visiting foreign specialists to the Owl so that they could eat *"real American food."* This is the kind of judgement you have to make for yourself, of course. And there are other places to eat in San Antonio, too.

# CARTHAGE

Going east out of San Antonio you are traveling on Highway 380. Eight and five tenths miles from the Owl Bar and Cafe, look to your right for a three strand, barb wire gate and a dirt road. You can go through this gate. (The Code of the West demands that you close every gate that you open, unless of course, you like chasing cattle on highways and paying angry ranchers for more dead beef than you could ever eat. Don't bother with going to court. In matters of gates and cattle, the New Mexico jury will always side with the rancher, the cattle, and the land; anyone else is a miscreant. Just close the gates. Firmly.) Follow the road and you will soon be at an old cemetery.

This old cemetery belonged to the mining town of Carthage, and the town of Carthage was once a major coal center. Three times Carthage developed into a boom town and three times it failed. The mining activity started in the 1880's and in the early years of the 1950's the coal mining equipment was taken out of the Carthage area and transferred to the mines at Madrid, New Mexico. At times the population of Carthage was in the thousands, and the town boasted hotels and schools and bars. By 1915 its population had shrunk to 415, and eventually all trace of activity ceased. Carthage, as a townsite, straggled all over the hills and on both sides of Highway 380. Carthage was named by an educated army officer who noted that it shared the same map coordinates as the ancient Greek city.

You can walk about and pick up shards of old purple glass, rusty nails and old abalone shirt buttons. The detrius of living is abundant. Perhaps the most poignant reminder of the life that was Carthage is in the old graveyard. Tombstones can be found inscribed in many languages. Entire families are laid to rest side by side. Men who fought in all of America's terrible wars were brought home to this isolated spot and laid in New Mexico soil under their veteran's headstones. And there are frequently fresh flowers on the neatly kept graves, and just as frequently another old wooden marker will finally give way and turn from a cross to a dry stick of wood on a grave that no one visits any more.

*Reflection — filled with rain, a small pool in the desert reflects an upthrust butte.*

In the sand hills below the graves, if you are keen-eyed and quiet, you might be able to spot one of the great horned owls that fly over the townsite. And in late August after the summer rains, if you go down to the groves of tamarisk and salt cedars that have turned into a marshy, mosquitoey spot, you may be witness to the Toad Phenomenon. A zillion quarter-sized toads will cover the ground. You will not want to walk around because of the carnage each foot will bring to the toad population. The cute little hoppers will be everywhere and you will swear that on your last visit here there was not any sign of toad life at all. Like Carthage, the toads appear and flourish briefly and disappear. Carthage is a bitter-sweet stop on a wanderer's way.

Back on the road, after closing the gate carefully behind you, you can head on to the east and venture to Carrizozo and out of the pages of this book. Or you can retrace your steps to San Antonio and continue south on the *"old road"* until it rejoins the Interstate at San Marcial. Or you could have taken the Interstate out of Socorro and got off at the San Antonio exit where you can now get back on, if you wish. But be a wanderer. Take the *old road* so that you can visit the Bosque Del Apache Wildlife Refuge.

## Bosque Del Apache Wildlife Refuge _____

Four miles south, out of San Antonio will bring you to the border of the Bosque Del Apache Wildlife Refuge. Start watching the tops of the power poles on either side of the road so that you will be able to see one of the great hawks that live in this area. The hawks seem to prefer these tee-shaped perches, and it isn't difficult to spot them as you drive by. Bosque means *"grove or thicket"* in Spanish and the Apache Indians used to campe or hide, depending on your point of view, in the tangle of trees that grew in this area. Modern agriculture has cleaned up the thicket somewhat, but the name remains.

Nine miles from San Antonio you will see the entrance to the Wildlife Refuge on your left. The admission is free, and you can pick up maps and brochures at a little information station just inside the gate. The refuge that is accessible by car, is a series of flooded fields, dikes, and thickets that are home to deer, pheasants, coyotes, quail, eagles, and many, many species of water fowl. In the late fall and all through the winter, the fields will be covered with sandhill cranes, ibsis, ducks of many kinds, grebes, and geese. The best time to see the wildlife population is at dawn and sunset. At these times the larger flying birds will be leaving for the morning feeding or returning for the evening stay. The sky will actually be dark with the flocks of birds, and the noise of their wings will be a roar. It is simply difficult to believe that there are so many birds in one spot. Take binoculars and a bird book. The tour through the Refuge is self-guided, and there is a small museum across the road from the entrance at the ranger station. You can't camp here. The place belongs to the wildlife.

## FORT CRAIG _____

You can either go back to San Antonio now and get on the Interstate or you can continue down the *"old road"* to the San Marcial entrance/exit and get on I-25 there. Once you are headed south, look to the left or east and you will be able to see a high mesa near the river. This is the area where Fort Craig stood. Established in 1855, it became the refuge for the defeated Union troops in the first battle of the Civil War fought in New Mexico. During a one day encounter, Confederate troops from Texas (one of the reasons New Mexicans distrust Texans) under General Sibley, overwhelmed the union troops at Valverde and then continued up the Rio Grande to capture Albuquerque and Santa Fe.

Visitors and history buffs can no longer travel by car to Fort Craig. The state is making efforts to develop it as a park and historical monument.

# SAN MARCIAL _____

Thirty miles south of Socorro and you are at San Marcial. There isn't a town here anymore. In the early days of New Mexico, the explorer, conquistador and adventurer, Onate designated this spot as Paraje de Fray Christobal. Fray Christobal was a priest in Onate's entourage, and the place was the last chance to get water before starting the *Journey of Death* across the dry, hot plains. Later, a small settlement grew on the west bank of the Rio Grande. It was called after San Marcial of France and it was destroyed by a flood in 1866. New San Marcial was then re-established on the west bank of the Rio Grande and was a stopping place for the railroad. The town was again inundated in 1929 and still the people remained. The post office held out until it was closed in 1944. When Elephant Butte Lake was built in the 1920's the original site of Paraje was covered by water. There is a great deal of history here and actually very little to see.

One time on a back-packing trip into the Magdalena mountains, Gilbert Phillips and I stood on the South Peak of those mountains and with a look of dreamy thought, Gilbert pointed out his hometown of Rosedale and San Marcial in the Rio Grande Valley, and he recounted to me how he and his father had taken a Model-T Ford from Rosedale to San Marcial on a sixty mile trek for supplies. San Marcial was the major trading point for the area in the early nineteen twenties. Now both Rosedale and San Marcial are mostly memories, and Gilbert lives in Albuquerque.

Back on the Interstate, the road will take the traveler through land that could be described as typically *"New Mexico of the South."* It is flat and wide and open. Mountains, blue and grey, decorate the edges where the land meets the sky. And the sky — the wide sky is endless and blue. From a car the land appears featureless, dotted with greasewood bushes and covered with grasses, rocks and gravel. An occasional bunch of cattle relieve the eye of monotony. The sweep is endless and magnificent.

## The Immigration Station

About one hundred and fifty miles from Albuquerque, you will come to a cluster of buildings on the left side of the highway. If there is any traffic going north, you will notice the cars stopping here as you go by. This is a Federal Immigration Station. The people who work here are agents controlling illegal immigration into the United States. In New Mexico this usually means preventing illegal aliens from Mexico from entering the state. If you are driving north, you must pass through this station where an agent in a green uniform will simply ask if you are a citizen and glance at your car to see if you are carrying illegal aliens in the back seat. If they catch any illegal aliens they put them into green busses with bars on the windows and drive them back to Mexico. Because of the green uniforms and green busses, the illegal aliens, aka *"wetbacks,"* call these federal agents *"aguacates"* or avocados. They probably call them other things, too. Mexico has the same type of setup on the highways into their country so they can check on who is entering their lands too.

# III

## Truth or Consequences
### Elephant Butte Dam and Reservoir
### Geronimo Springs Museum

# TRUTH OR CONSEQUENCES

The highway will take you on to Truth or Consequences. Get off the Interstate at the first exit so you can see the entire town. T or C, as many call it is a very interesting, pleasant place with a wealth of activities for the wanderer. Before you come to the highway exit for the town proper, you will see exits for Elephant Butte Dam and Reservoir.

Elephant Butte Lake State Park and Recreation Area and Caballo Lake, below Elephant Butte, are big recreation areas. There is camping, boating, water skiing, sailing, swimming, and canoeing. The way to these places is clearly marked and if the weather is at all warm, you are bound to encounter scores of people busy having fun. These places do not appeal to my wandering heart. They have their share of folklore and history, and you may have a very enjoyable time exploring here. When you are finished, the road will be awaiting you.

Truth or Consequences is the town which was once called Hot Springs. In the early nineteen fifties, the popular radio show, Truth or Consequences advertised for an American town that was willing to change its name to Truth or Consequences to honor the show's tenth anniversary. Besides being a popular show, Truth or Consequences was noted for its efforts in raising money for nationwide charities like the March of Dimes and the American Cancer Society. The reward for changing the town's name was national recognition and an annual festival when the Truth or Consequences radio show would be broadcast from that city.

Hot Springs, New Mexico was selected out of the towns and cities which bid for the recognition, and in 1951 it officially became known as Truth or Consequences, New Mexico. Although the radio show eventually went off the air and reappeared as a television program, which also passed on, Ralph Edwards and his wife faithfully show up each year at T or C and the town has a big fiesta with parades, barbeques, boat races, and dances.

Of course there are some people who think this is all a lot of malarky and they insist on calling the place Hot Springs, but almost everyone knows they mean Truth or Consequences. Many of the residents are very proud of their town and their fiesta, and they regard Mr. and Mrs. Edwards as neighbors or friends who happen to be gone most of the time.

Before the name change, Hot Springs was a locally known landmark because it actually does have remarkable, natural hot springs. These springs do not smell, come bubbling out of the ground, and are said to be very effective for relieving arthritis pain. Others think that drinking the mineral water is good for the digestive tract. There are private bath houses all over Hot Springs, and a hot mineral bath can be just the thing to soothe a weary wanderer. They aren't generally expensive and the water is usually between 97 and 114 degrees. Watch for signs or ask someone who looks like they live here. In the summer the town is full of people who have come to enjoy the nearby lake. These people are easily recognizable as non-residents by their sunburns, so ask someone else.

## Geronimo Springs Museum

Geronimo Springs Museum is located on your right as you drive south through Truth or Consequences. It is a new looking brick building with arches built into the brick work, and standing next to it is a smaller, roofed, brick grotto with some rocks inside and a hot spring bubbling forth. This is the Geronimo Hot Spring where Geronimo and his Apache warriors were known to stop to soothe their wounds. It is available to the public.

The museum is run by the Sierra County Historical Society. The people in the Society are well informed about their area and have made a grand effort to gather up and present items that show the visitor what living in this area means. Many of the members lived their lives in the surrounding countryside, and have contributed artifacts that make the past seem very close.

This museum is a museum for people and brought into existence by people. It is not backed by major institutions, but by the interest of people. Look carefully at everything here. There may be much that doesn't interest or impress you, but there is sure to be something that will capture your attention and make you glad you spent some time wandering here.

The museum is very dense. Not only is there a lot to see, but everything has been given equal importance. This lets the museum visitor ponder for him/herself exactly how and why each exhibit was important to the history of the land. It's the ultimate self-guided museum trip, and it is exactly the type of place a wanderer would delight in. If you have any questions, the docents on duty can usually help you and they turn out to be friends, neighbors, or relatives of the actual contributors of the displays. The museum is divided into four categories; Natural Resources, Historical Past, Ralph Edwards and the T or C Fiesta, and the Cultural Heritage room.

The Cultural Heritage room gave me one of the biggest surprises I have ever received while wandering New Mexico. First, the Cultural Heritage room is easy to miss. After viewing the museum proper, passing the gift shop which has one of the most extensive selections of books about New Mexico that I have ever seen, you must go through the community room where the residents of T or C may be playing bridge or having a meeting, go on through the Ralph Edwards room, and finally you are in the Cultural Heritage room. When I first stepped into this room I stood and simply gawked.

The walls are lined with four wall-to-ceiling murals depicting four men who made noteable contributions to the area. The murals are alive with color and done in a formal, classical style that you don't expect after viewing the informal exhibits in the rest of the museum. The artist, Delmas Howe was born in Truth or Consequences, and his work is displayed in public buildings all across the nation.

In the center of the room are four bronze busts, again of four famous New Mexicans. These were sculpted by Hivana Leyendecker, another native New Mexican, and again they are not what you expected to see in the Cultural Heritage room. They are the work of an accomplished master artist, and a pleasure to view.

Back on the road again, head south out of town. As you reach the outskirts of T or C, start looking to your left for a large building, set well off the road, fronted by a large lawn. There will be no sign identifying this building. It used to be the Carrie Tingley Hospital for Crippled Children. For many years it was a major orthopedic center for children in the Southwest. It moved to the regional medical center in Albuquerque at the end of the nineteen seventies. Carrie Tingley was the wife of Governor Clyde Tingley, and was dedicated to helping sick and handicapped children. She is known as a lady who made a difference in New Mexico.

Just beyond the old hospital you will enter the community of Williamsburg. It is a suburb of Truth or Consequences. After Hot Springs changed its name to T or C, Williamsburg used the name of Hot Springs for a while, but eventually went back to being Williamsburg. From here you will be able to get back on the Interstate and continue down the road.

# IV

# Socorro to Truth or Consequences

## by way of:

The Langmuir Observatory

Magdalena

Kelly

Riley

Rosedale

Winston

Cuchillo

In Socorro, if you choose not to go east to San Antonio and the Bosque Del Apache, you can go west and visit Magdalena and the ghost towns of Riley, Kelly and Rosedale. Turn right, off the main street of Socorro when you see the sign and the arrow directing you to Highway 60. On my last trip there was a vacant lot on this corner to help you identify it. One time there was a tent revivalist there with his tent pitched and his loudspeakers ready to save souls. Although I waited patiently for several hours, and the preacher waited impatiently, no one showed up at that corner to be saved. It remains a poignant picture in my memory: the minister in the doorway of his lighted tent and the soft, summer darkness falling over the vacant lot. I remembered his name for a long time, but I've forgotten it now.

Magdalena is thirty-odd miles from Socorro. It is a short drive, but it can be thrilling because the sharp-eyed observer may spot the antelope herd that lives in the flatlands on the right side of the highway. Many people aren't excited by these graceful little creatures but they are among the last wild herd animals to roam freely in this part of the world. In the past, spotting an antelope herd was important because it meant meat and food. When I speak of the past here, it is not the distant-Wild-West-past, but the last forty or fifty years.

## The Langmuir Observatory

About sixteen miles out of Socorro is the turn-off to Water Canyon. This road will also lead you to the Langmuir Observatory in the Magdalena Mountains. This isolated research station, high in the mountains, is involved in the investigation of lightning. Located in an area of great lightning fields, it is one spot in the U.S. where lightning strikes more than almost anywhere else.

## MAGDALENA

As you come into Magdalena you will see an imposing brick house presiding over a hilltop on your left. It was built in the grand old tradition by a successful man for his bride. And in the equally grand tradition of tragedy, she did not live long to enjoy it. However, Gilbert Phillips' aunts did live there at one time, and after a visit to them he told me this story about the pleasures they enjoyed as children in Magdalena.

All over the Southwest there grows a plant called Angel's Trumpet by some, and datura or sacred datura by others. It is a large sprawling plant, and when it blooms it carries big, graceful, trumpet-shaped, white flowers. Datura is extremely poisonous and dangerous and it also has the same mind altering abilities as other psycho-active materials like magic mushrooms or LSD. Gilbert recalled that as a child, his aunt told him he could take the flowers and squeeze them into his eyes and then for a couple of hours "things would sure look funny." She seemed to think it was perfectly appropriate knowledge for a child, and Gilbert did it. He says things did look funny, and as a child it was a pretty interesting thing to do. **Don't try this!** This is dangerous. Sacred datura is also called jimson weed, which is a diminutive of

*Sacred Datura — tightly furled bud of the plant encloses the flower that can bring death or visions.*

Jamestown weed. In the first colony of Jamestown, on the eastern seaboard, the people tried to eat this plant with the nice white root and they died.

There is a mountain range that seems to intrude right into Magdalena. These are the Magdalena Mountains! On the north end, as you drive into the town, you may see the head and shoulders of a woman outlined on the mountain side. This is Mary Magdalene, and she is said to have performed various miracles for people in need here. The picture is formed by rocks and brush and it takes a bit of gazing to pick it out. Sometimes just at sunset and just at sunrise it stands out boldly.

Magdalena used to be a major shipping point for cattle ranchers in New Mexico. They got supplies here and sent their cattle east to the packing plants in Chicago from here. Magdalena is mentioned in both Zane Grey's stories and Louise L'Amour's books. It is quiet now. It does have its moments though, when the past is remembered. In the summer the citizens of Magdalena celebrate their past with a parade, a barbeque and a rodeo. It is a very American celebration with a marching band and pretty girls and lots and lots of horses and floats. A queen is selected to reign and the rodeo offers good prizes. There is one thing that makes this occasion unique. All the queen candidates and all of the rodeo competitors have to be over sixty.

There is nothing that will make you feel quite so out-of-shape as watching a seventy-two year old man on a horse rope a calf and hogtie him. And stand up and not be breathing hard. These acts command your respect as does the sight of every work-hardened elderly person there. These are the people who settled the west. They held the land. They accomplished in their daily lives things that many people today would declare impossible or dangerous. Try to wander by for this community celebration. It's a big chapter in New Mexico's history.

Smithsonite is another thing that makes this part of New Mexico unique. Smithsonite is a semi-precious mineral that is found in association with zinc. It is a delicate blue-green color and it is opaque. Very occasionally it can be found with a rosy pink tint, but this is rare indeed. Smithsonite was named for the founder of the Smithsonian Institute and it can be found only in Kelly, New Mexico and one mine in Mexico. Smithsonite is 45 percent zinc and is very heavy. It is sold by the carat, like diamonds. Look up the Otero family in Magdalena if you want some Smithsonite. Although the mines at Kelly are closed and are forbidden to all comers, the Oteros used to work there and they have a glorious selection of Smithsonite for sale.

# KELLY

Kelly is only two miles south of Magdalena. Turn left at the marked intersection that is past the Ranger Station. It is a dirt road, but perfectly driveable.

In its heyday, Kelly was a town of more than three thousand people. Their lives revolved around the mining industry and the mines at Kelly had an unusually fine grade of zinc and lead ore. The town was in existence for seventy-five years. During that time it had a large hotel, McDonald's general store, public schools, and all the other services for a community that large. Although a bit of silver mining was done here in the 1800's, the primary mineral was zinc. Kelly was making arrangements to ship zinc to Germany before World War I broke out and as a result, only one box car of the ore was ever exported.

As you approach the townsite, you will see wide and low concrete structures on either side of the road. These are all that remain of the Pittsburgh Paint Company's refining operation that used to be a part of the Kelly economy.

Park by the small church and walk up the road to a ramshackley gate. No one is supposed to enter the town, but after a rain you will be able to see many of Magdalena's citizens walking around on the high dumps that are to your left by the abandoned mine entrance. They are looking for Smithsonite washed free by the rain.

The road winds past McDonald's store and the old hotel, but all you can see are crumbling walls. Weeds are growing everywhere. If you stay on the old road, you can walk a mile or so, to the Old Jaunita Mine. The road is very steep but easily walkable. During the spring, summer, and fall there will always be some kind of wild flower blooming and enlivening the landscape.

If you pause on the way and look down on the quiet, empty hollow it is difficult to believe that anyone ever called this home. there is so little left. Yet, in the mid-nineteen-twenties, a small boy was living in Kelly and a prospector with his burro came to the door of his home. After a brief conversation with the head of the house, the small boy was sent with the prospector to McDonald's store. The boy was to carry the message that the household would stand for the prospector's grubstake. While supplies were being gathered in the store, the little boy waited to escort the old miner back home. At one point, the storekeeper went off to a backroom and the wide-eyed little boy saw the old prospector slip a single, large onion into his overcoat pocket. With a dark and menacing look, the burly prospector put a finger to his lips and signaled the boy to keep still. The prospector eventually went to his reward but the boy kept his secret until he was a grown man of fifty-six. It somehow seems all right to tell the tale now.

## The Juanita Mine —

Entering old mines is extremely dangerous and no one should attempt it. The Juanita is dark and cool and scary inside. It is so narrow it is difficult to believe that men came here on a daily basis to earn their living. Only the wildlife creatures have any real reason to enter the Juanita now.

Standing by the Juanita, facing north, you will be confronted by an extremely steep hillside. This you must climb to reach a high ridge on the top of the hill. Following the ridge to your right and then north will eventually lead you to the old Ambrosia mine. This is a rugged all-day hike and should not be attempted without a gallon of water and a topographical map.

## The Ambrosia Mine —

Once at the dizzy heights of the Ambrosia you will see the town of Magdalena laid out with careful precision. Looking closely on the ground around the entrance to the Ambrosia you may be able to find some gem-quality chryscola. But even without the mineral, the view is worth the trip.

The Ambrosia is another dark and dangerous mine. Do not enter it. The Ambrosia is unique among mines. You can stand at the west entrance and view Magdalena, enter the mine, walk the shaft and exit at the east with a view to Strawberry Hill. (Strawberry Hill is a technical rock climbers delight.) The Ambrosia is not extensive but it pierces the ridge completely. The timbers in the Ambrosia invoke awe. They are not too massive, only about 15 inches in diameter but each one is approximately 25 feet long. This means that they were hauled to the top of this narrow, rocky ridge by mules and maneuvered whole into the twisting mine shaft. It took two and maybe three little pack animals to bring up one timber that would be used to shore up the Ambrosia, and the critters did not come up the way described in the previous pages. They walked up the west side of the mountain to the mouth of the Ambrosia.

Also on the east side is the crumbling blacksmithy. Every mine had its own forge and blacksmith, and the Ambrosia is no exception. Little remains of it now and the place is overrun with straw-colored scorpions.

Gold has an amazing power to motivate man. The lure of gold can really bring forth a person's creative abilities. The Ambrosia is proof of this.

On the way back from the Ambrosia make sure you keep drinking water; the high altitude will be cool and will trick you into thinking you have not lost moisture from your exertions. The Magdalena Mountains are not the place to be found dehydrated, if anyone can find you.

Retrace your steps to Magdalena. If you drive around the town you may see a house painted on the outside with designs from Navajo rugs. This is the home of Peter Klinefelter. Klinefelter retired to Magdalena from a job in the East and is now devoting his time to painting artistic, yet photographically accurate, paintings of ancient Mimbres pottery. Owning a Klinefelter is almost like owning one of these rare and beautiful pots. On occasion he may paint a rodeo scene or a wild turkey or some other wildlife, but his renderings of the pottery are riveting.

# RILEY

Riley is another small spot in New Mexico that is a monument to mankind's tenacity. People put down roots and establish homes or ranches and then they stay and stay. Floods, droughts, and hard times do not move them. They have children and the children stay. Brothers and sisters *"move to town"* and come back. This is the history of Riley.

To go there, take the Riley road out of Magdalena. This is the road that goes north that is NOT Highway 52. About twenty miles from Magdalena, the road will end on the banks of the Rio Salado, and depending on the season and the amount of water in the river, you will be able to drive across and pick up the road on the far side.

Once in Riley you will be able to wander the dusty street and pick out the school house and the church. The church is a very old building, and the original was a small mission built by early Catholic fathers. There is a small graveyard in front of the church, and even today, the native sons and daughters request to be placed there for the final rest. Riley is not yet a ghost town, although it is crumbling into dust as the years pass. In the spring there will be apple trees blooming among the old adobe buildings and it will seem a lovely spot. In the summer it is blisteringly hot and the absence of water is a nagging worry.

A priest still comes every month to say mass in the old church and the residents of Riley, past and present, hold a reunion every May. Everyone is welcome at this fiesta and it is a perfect time to hear first-hand about the life in early New Mexico.

I used to drive out to Riley and visit a man named Daniel Bustamente. He had lived in Riley as a young man and later came back. His tombstone in the churchyard shows that he was a war veteran, but he never spoke of that. Instead he told me stories of his youth and the sheep camps and cattle drives where he worked. He rode a powerful white horse then, and he must have been a handsome sight on that white horse with his coal black hair and flashing eyes. Daniel Bustamente lived here in Riley with his sister and the wide sky; I lived in a bustling city and we liked each other. I'm sorry he is not still here.

If you leave Riley on the road that goes north, you will eventually end up back in Bernardo. If you watch carefully as you drive along, you will see the line shacks set off the road, away from the traffic. These small buildings usually hold an iron bed and a stove, and they were built for the cowboys who rode the boundaries checking the fences. Line shacks aren't too common anymore because most cowboys ride in pickup trucks and can always get back to the ranch by bedtime.

About five miles outside of Riley, going north, you will be going through some low hills that hug either side of the road. Standing atop one of these hills is a statue of the Virgin. If you are not watching it will flash by and you will miss this symbol in the desert. If you should park your car and climb up to this image you will find a burned out votive candle and perhaps a plastic flower or two. Whoever comes to pray at this out-of-the-way spot must have a compelling reason.

Further down the road, on the west or left hand side, is a small gypsum and bat cave. This cave is not as dangerous as an abandoned mine. Most of its danger comes from the reptiles that like to sleep in the cool, or the fact that the bats may have rabies. Weigh your chances before you decide to enter. Be alert.

Retrace your trip to Magdalena. If you are hungry now, look for Crucitas Cafe on the west end of town on the main road. If Crucitas is open, stop for a meal. If you are not an experienced chile eater, the combination plate will give you a good idea of what Mexican food is all about. The prices are great and the food is too. After your meal you are ready to go on to Rosedale.

# ROSEDALE

Rosedale is a small ghost town that once clustered around a gold mine. Take the road leaving Magdalena to the south. This is State Road 107. About twenty-seven miles from Magdalena, you will see a sign on the right directing you to "Grassy Mountain Lookout." Take this turn-off to the right. It is a dirt road but very passable. As you go along, start looking to your right. Very soon you will see a neatly fenced graveyard and a few old houses. Once you spot the old mine works (they are quite far off the road, but visable from it) you are in Rosedale. If you get out and walk around, look for the large patches of dirt where no plants are growing. These barren spots are the environmental ignorance that mark Rosedale.

Rosedale had the type of mining operation that used arsenic to extract the gold from the mined ore. Arsenic was carried into Rosedale in great sacks and stored around the mill. There were no safeguards. The waste from the extraction process was *"thrown away."* Rain carried spilled arsenic into the soil and into the community. One resident of Rosedale remembers that all the children were told not to drink the water that ran across the ground. Drink only the water that was carried into the settlement and was therefore safe. But tragedy was inevitable. A healthy little cousin was last seen playing happily. The next time anyone saw the child he was dead and the only explanation was that he must have gotten thirsty playing and stopped to drink the water in a small creek that ran nearby.

Arsenic was a known danger, but it was not controlled. Either cost or ignorance prevented the mine operators from careful handling of this deadly poison. The cost then was human lives and the cost now seems to be sterility in the land. Did the mine operators have any idea what would happed to the soil as a result of their industry?

But Rosedale was not all tragedy. The people who lived there worked hard, but they played hard too. When a dance was announced in the community center, everyone came. Babies were laid on blankets on the floor and the dancing went on all night. No one stopped until the musicians either gave out or the sun came up. Because of community pressure, the musicians learned to play in shifts and usually it was the dawn that ended the dances.

Return to the sign that directed you to Grassy Mountain Lookout. If you turn to the right and continue to the south, you will have a pleasant drive of about twelve miles before State Road 107 delivers you back to the Interstate at the Fort Craig-San Marcial area. From here you can continue on to Truth or Consequences.

However, if you want to go to Truth or Consequences by a longer and infinitely more interesting route, take a left and follow State Road 107 back to the north about ten miles. At this point a small gravel road will branch to your left. Follow it for twelve miles and you will connect with State Road 52. (Of course you could have skipped the trip to Rosedale and picked up State Road 52 twelve miles out of Magdalena. A wanderer's life is full of decisions!)

This route is a great example of the way that New Mexico manages to pack a multitude of different landscapes into a seventy-five mile drive. Once on State Road 52, you will begin by driving across vast stretches of range land. This is where all those beefsteaks come from. The land is lovely and the space will make your spirits soar. This is also a good stretch of road to bird watch for the small falcons known as kestrels. They are abundant here. Look for them on the telephone poles.

The gravel road will continue and the countryside will gently change until you are passing through rolling hills. You will drive into small valleys and out, and see picturesque windmills and small trees. This part of the trip is called the *Valley of Flowers* because in the autumn the flowers will be the primary object on display. There will just be a whole bunch of 'em. Every color — every kind — everywhere. Write your own poem. (This is not marked on any map I have ever read, but it is there all the same. The benefits of being a wanderer are discoveries like this.)

Eventually the road will take you up a very steep climb. The road will be narrow and rocky. When you reach the top you will begin a descent into Bear Trap Canyon. This is National Forest land and you will now be in a Ponderosa pine forest. A little stream will wander along the road and you will see it sparkling in the sunlight. If it is not a weekend or holiday, the camping here is idyllic; quiet and tranquil under the tall pines.

Driving on, the road will now start to rise again and you will be on a very high, wind-swept mesa. Again the land will roll away from you to blue mountains in the far distance. The contrast between the cozy pines and the demanding expanse of mesa land is confusing. This is unconventional beauty.

## CUCHILLO and WINSTON _____

The road goes on and it eventually will start to descend. Highway 59 will join 52, but drive on. The land now goes flat and the road follows the Cuchillo Negro *"Black Knife"* River into Winston. Cuchillo Negro was an Apache contemporary of Geronimo. Once in Winston you are 28 miles from T or C. Keep on the road and you will pass small ranch houses and large cattle herds. The land here is gentler. There is evidence of civilization and people. In about 16 miles you will run into Cuchillo. After this, the road will take you across twelve miles of the flattest, mesquite-covered land in New Mexico. Every mile looks like every other mile and it will easily lull you to sleep. If you are lucky though, you may cross this in a thunder storm. In this case, you will be the audience for spectacular displays of lightning that seem to be striking RIGHT IN FRONT OF YOU! RIGHT BEHIND YOU! OVER TO THE LEFT! OVER TO THE RIGHT! Get out your camera and try to remember how to take pictures of this. The drive will be over before you know it. Welcome to T or C.

# V.
# Truth or Consequences to Deming
### via
### Hillsboro
### and Nutt

Once out of Williamsburg you CAN get back on Interstate 25. Stay on this and it will shoot you down to Las Cruces and El Paso. But a far more enjoyable way south is over the Black Range Mountains. The jumping-off spot for a trip across the Black Range is Hillsboro, nestled at the foot of the Black Range.

Don't get back on the Interstate. Stay on the main road out of Williamsburg which is old Highway 85. Roll along this fine old road passing Las Palomas. Soon you will see a dirt road running under the freeway and a sign that marks Animas Creek. Follow this road.

## The Animas Creek Suspension Bridge _____

It is pleasant to drive up this gravel track and catch glimpses of little homesteads, log cabins and startlingly modern structures. Mailboxes announce the names of the inhabitants and in true wanderer's style you begin to wonder what it would be like to live here. The road is tree-lined and wild-flowery in season. It can also be muddy instead of dusty.

This little side trip will also give the wanderer a chance to practice the New Mexico road greeting; when another truck approaches, nod pleasantly and lift two or three fingers from the steering wheel. Do all of this in time for the other driver to see it. They will be doing the same thing. If you don't do this, they will know that you did not grow up in rural New Mexico or that you are a surly son-of-a-bitch.

After twisting and turning for several miles you will come to a spot where the Animas Creek crosses the road. There is an old-style suspension foot bridge here. These wonderful bridges are rarely built anymore and this one is a classic.

Of course, the people who built this bridge and those who use it and maintain it, have very good reasons for doing so. People on the other side of the bridge are living and working and loving. They have little folk who must cross the Animas when it is flooding in order to get to school in T or C or Las Cruces. There are people who must buy groceries, go to doctors and business offices who also use the bridge. You will be able to see one of their cars parked on THIS side of the bridge while another car is parked on the FAR side of the bridge. There is life on the other side of that suspension bridge. Depending on the amount of water in Animas Creek, this may be your turn-around point. It was mine.

## COPPER FLATS

Back on the Interstate, start watching for the Highway 90 turn-off to Hillsboro. Make your turn and you are on your way. The two-lane blacktop stretches straight across the desert with telephone poles on either side. This road can be a surrealistic experience at the *"blue hour"* right around sundown. In fact, this road is so straight and so flat that the State Highway Department has done the traveler the courtesy of putting up signs to announce the few dips that appear in the road. The blue mountains ahead of you move up fast and before you know it the flat is behind you and the road is rising into hills.

There is not much evidence of people in these hills, but at one time there was a prospector with a claim on every one. Watch to your right and you will spot a cluster of small towers and a few buildings. This is the big Copper Flats project that was initiated in the late nineteen-seventies when copper prices were high. For a few years, the high price of copper made mining low-grade copper ore profitable. Copper Flats was built at this time and everyone was ready to see Hillsboro boom again. But the price of copper dropped before the Copper Flats operation could ever be put on line and like so many mining ventures in this country, the dream faded and failed.

The road now goes through a looping, winding course and the desert turns into softly contoured hills. Rolling into Hillsboro you've gone eighteen miles from the highway.

## HILLSBORO

Hillsboro has been in existence since the early 1870's. It was primarily a mining town and it was the home base for many miners. The stage lines ran through Hillsboro and it was the county seat until 1937 when T or C got the honor. During its heydays, an estimated six million dollars of gold and silver were taken from the mines in the hills in this area. The mines had romantic and fanciful names such as "The Bridal Chamber" and the "Silver King."

Presiding over Hillsboro was a lady named Sadie Orchard. There are many tales about Sadie. She was the first

woman stagecoach driver and she owned a saloon and boarding house. Some say she was no lady and also was in charge
of the prostitutes who worked in Hillsboro. No matter what
the truth, Sadie was a presence in Hillsboro. When you visit
the Black Range Museum in Hillsboro, (it's the first one you
come to, on the east side of town) you will get a glimpse of
the forceful personality that was Sadie Orchard. You will
also get a more elusive and perhaps more tantalizing glimpse
of a Chinese gentleman who was also a presence in this town.
Time after time this man appears in the history of Hillsboro
and you have to wonder who he really was and how he got to
New Mexico from China. There is also the elusive quality of
his relationship with Sadie Orchard. Were they simply
employer and employee, as he worked as a cook for her
establishments? Were they friends or business partners? Did
she front businesses for him because of his lack of English?
Were they lovers? Hillsboro was a town of thousands and
Sadie lived there at a time when there were few women in the
business world. She might have been a lonely woman,
belonging to neither the population of respectable ladies or
the sisterhood of "fancy ladies." Someone might know the
answers to these questions, but I haven't found them yet.

There are other spots of interest and history in Hillsboro.
At one time the daughter of the outlaw *"Doc Holliday"* was
running a tiny guest house there. There are antique stores and
a saloon. The people in Hillsboro are interested in the history
and most of them will tell you what they remember. By any
measure, Hillsboro was a colorful and active place. You
could probably buy or sell just about anything in Hillsboro,
and at one time Lillian Russell appeared there.

Hillsboro is not without its tragic history. It is subject to
floods from the overflowing Percha Creek. At flood time the
population takes to the old schoolhouse on the hill above the
town. During one of the more recent floods, the local sheriff
lost his life while trying to check on the ladies who had
sought safety in the church. That was the time when brush,
carried by running water, stacked up against the bridge and
created the flood conditions in Hillsboro.

In the fall, usually on the long Labor Day weekend,
Hillsboro holds an Apple Festival. I could never quite figure
this out because I was never aware of a great many apple
trees in Hillsboro, but maybe they are there. Anyway the
town puts on this festival and it is one of the best examples of

small town cooperation that I have ever enjoyed. There is a flea market along the main street. There is a Bake House full of wonderful apple deserts like apple pan dowdy and apple tarts and apple pie and apple cobbler. The ladies who bake these things really know their way around an apple. There are square dances and fiddlers' contests. There is a street dance at night. If you enjoy this kind of pleasure, you'll enjoy the Hillsboro Apple Festival.

After savoring Hillsboro, you have to make a decision: will you go over the Black Range and through Emory Pass on Highway 90 or will you leave Hillsboro on Highway 27 and head south for Nutt?

## Hillsboro to Deming via Nutt_____

Half way through Hillsboro there is a road on the left that climbs the hill to the schoolhouse and then branches left again. This is Highway 27 and it will take you south thirty-four miles to meet Highway 26 at Nutt, New Mexico. These thirty-odd miles offer the most extraordinary scenery in New Mexico. In any season that you pass through this land you will be witness to what may be some of the most severely beautiful land in America. You will see vast oceans of grass rolling up to meet a turquoise sky. There will be rounded hills and rugged mountains. Dry water courses, with arrangements of boulders and twisted oaks, look as if they would be at home in a Zen garden. Horses group themselves picturesquely on the crowns of hills and far and away the ranch houses hide in the hollows. Whenever I take this drive I am gripped by the illogical but demanding desire for the land; owning it, working it, living on it. Since I can only possess it visually, I return again and again for satisfaction.

## The Enchanted Ocotillo Forest and the Valley of the Wasp _____

Fifteen miles out of Hillsboro you will see a State Highway milepost that reads 15. Approximately one half mile south of this start looking and you might be able to see a terrible dirt road angling off to the right from the highway and disappearing into a small slit between two high hills. This road is in the in-between area; the land is changing between the hills of Hillsboro and meadowy land of Lake Valley. If you are willing to torture your car and endanger your oil pan, take this road. About a quarter of a mile up it you will begin to see plastic water pipe running beside the road. This is the only indication you will have that you are on the road that I am thinking of. The road is VERY STEEP. It is a VERY BAD road. However, as it rises up to a mesa you will begin to notice a lush growth of cactus and wildflowers and desert plants of every species. You will never reach the mesa. You might get as far as the stock tank. The plastic pipe has something to do with this. If you are sincerely intrepid or merely dumb or adventurous, you can continue on until the road is gone and there is a deep ravine on the right and a sloping hill on the left. This is a natural botanical garden and a spot of quiet beauty. This is the Enchanted Ocotillo Forest. In the spring there will be round and red hedgehog cactus. In the late summer there is a profusion of red-tipped Ocotillo, also known as the Devil's Riding Whip. There are yuccas and chamisa. It is an amazing array of plant types.

Uncork a bottle of your traveling wine and sit down to enjoy the sunset. Be ready for the visit (informal) from the wasps that live in this area. Do not flail about and frighten them. They are only curious and they will not harm you unless you harm them. After a bit they will get bored and leave or the sun will set and they will leave. Wasps don't have a big nightlife.

After sundown you may be lucky and hear the coyote song. Coyote songs are getting to be rather rare because the ranchers and other stockmen are very efficient at poisoning and killing the coyotes. There are good reasons on each side of the coyote controversy and a guidebook is not the forum for it. Simply savour the song if you can hear it.

Getting out of the Enchanted Forest and The Valley of the Wasp may be harder than getting in. But if you are a wanderer, you have frequently been in the position of not having any room to turn around. You know how to get your car out better than I do. The guide will carry on back at the highway.

A little more than half way through the drive, you will pass Lake Valley. Hidden in a fold of the hills, this was once another booming mining town. There was also once a lake here but it is gone now, too. During Lake Valley's short history, several attempts were made to give it other names, but people always referred to it as Lake Valley. Bodies of water always impress New Mexicans. Even when the lake went dry, the name remained.

In the late 1880's, Lake Valley was among the richest silver producing areas of the USA. In just six years it is estimated that the value of the silver dug out of the earth here was more than four million dollars. And that estimate is figured in 1880 dollars, which today would be many times that amount.

Finally, as you drive along you will reach Nutt. Nutt seems a little self conscious about its place in the universe these days. In the past it was much larger and more important. All the silver from this area was carted to Nutt and shipped by rail to the refineries. Without the railhead at Nutt, history might have been different. Turn right at Nutt and you will be heading south and slightly west on Highway 26. It's about thirty miles to Deming and after the scenery you just went through, the next miles will be nice but not spectacular. However, your senses might need a rest, having just been in visual overdrive during the Hillsboro to Nutt trek.

Just where Highway 26 meets Highway 180, outside of Deming, look for a produce stand. If it's the season for fresh fruits and vegetables you can usually pick up some nice produce here. The prices are reasonable and the people will respond to you in Spanish or English. They are very accommodating and let you pick the language of commerce. If you have been camping along your wanderer's way, it's probably time to stock up on something fresh so as to avoid scurvy. If you are planning on the excursion to Columbus you might do a little serious shopping here. Fresh produce is not the main attraction of Columbus. If it's winter, just drive on. Deming has great grocery stores, exactly like the ones back home.

# VI
# Hillsboro to Deming

### via

### Kingston

### The Gila Cliff Dwellings

### The Copper Domain

### Silver City

### Santa Rita

### Bayard

### Hurley

### City of Rocks

If you do not care to go to Deming by way of Nutt, you may choose the longer, more mountainous and possibly more historic route by remaining on Highway 90 as it passes through Hillsboro.

# KINGSTON

Nine miles outside of Hillsboro is another old mining town called Kingston. The residents of Kingston are making some effort to develop this old town as a tourist attraction, so from time to time you may find mining exhibits, antique shops or rock shops to visit. Silver was the precious metal mined in Kingston and the town got its name from the nearby Iron King mine. There were so many men in Kingston that at one time a single saloon carried eighty-one brands of whiskey.

Although the mines that were owned by the big companies made the history books, these mountains are pocketed with proprietor mines. Small operations that made good money for their owners and small crews are on every hillside. With names like the Silver Eagle, Long Feather, and Grey Owl, these little mines still haunt the imagination of modern prospectors who continue to stake and file claims, looking for another rich vein of silver or gold. Someday the boom will come again — somewhere — sometime — some dream.

As the road goes on, the countryside changes into pine and evergreen forests and the road starts to climb and curve sharply. A judicious toot on your car horn at the blind curves may relieve your mind and inform some speedster coming from the opposite direction that you are at the curve, too. The less timid can just drive.

During the late summer and early fall you will be entertained by the wildflowers. Unlike the mesas where you are treated to carpets of color, the mountain blooms will be small and individual; actually more enchanting in a small way. Red accents are frequently Indian Paintbrush and yellow accents can be anything. Botanists estimate that two-thirds of the world's flowers are yellow composites. (A composite is a flower built like a daisy with the petals arranged in a circle around a center.)

The road leading you upward is heading for Emory Pass. This path through the high Black Range is over 8000 feet above sea level. From the top of the pass, you have a wonderful, unobstructed view of the land. There is a National Forest Lookout at the top and it is nice to stop, park and look out. The Forest Service has placed a large, panoramic photograph here with all of the major landmarks labeled. You can stand in front of this picture, look at it, look out at the landscape and get yourself oriented. It's a simple thing, but it is something that the Forest Service has done very neatly.

## The Kneeling Nun

My favorite piece of geography in this part of the world is the Kneeling Nun. Shortly after leaving Emory Pass, look south and west out towards Cook's Range. You will be able to see a free-standing tower of rock sticking up in front of the flat face of that mountain range. By judicious use of your imagination, this will look like a woman in robes, a nun, kneeling in front of an altar. The story goes that a young nun who was nursing a sick or wounded soldier, fell in love with her patient. The nun left her vows, her sisters, and her church to be with the man she loved. To pay for this sin, the nun was to have spent eternity on her knees, begging for forgiveness. And so she kneels in the New Mexican landscape. A very serious thing — sin. At least to some.

Continuing the descent from Emory Pass, the road will go down through the pines until it meets Highway 61 at San Lorenzo. At this junction you have three choices. You can go to your right and travel north and west on Highways 61 and 15 to the Gila Cliff Dwellings. Or you can go west to Santa Rita, Central, Tyrone, Bayard, and Hurley and get a taste of the more recent history of mining in New Mexico. Or finally, you can opt out of history altogether and turn left, traveling the seventeen miles to the eerie tranquility of the City of Rocks State Park. The history of the City of Rocks has very little to do with homo sapiens.

## The Gila Cliff Dwellings

Turn right at San Lorenzo onto Highway 61. About twenty-one miles down this road, you will meet Highway 15. Again turn right. There will be a sign advising you that you are on your way to the Gila Cliff Dwellings and Visitor Center.

Before you reach the Cliff Dwellings however, you will see a turn-off to Lake Roberts. This is a pleasant little detour along the way and is an ideal spot for a picnic lunch.

The Cliff Dwellings are part of the National Monument system. There are three clusters of abandoned dwellings here and the park personnel are very much involved with preserving them. The dwellings are fragile.

The original inhabitants living here were agriculturalists raising beans, corn and vegetables in their fields which were located away from the village site. They were said to have lived short lives of only about 30 or 35 years. It was their custom to bury their dead in the floors of the rooms, usually curled up in a knees-to-chest chin-to-knees position. The dead were usually accompanied by some food and water for the journey to the Other World. In many cases, here and in other parts of the Southwest, a few personal belongings were also put into the grave. If pottery was included in the funerary pieces, the pots were always broken. The ancient Mimbres pottery is a good example of this. This pottery is most generally found with a small neat hole in the bottom of each piece. Modern day people can only conjecture about this custom and try to draw conclusions by comparing it with the practices and beliefs of modern day Native Americans.

The concensus about this is that the pottery was punctured to *"release"* the spirit of the owner or the maker. If the owner or the maker's spirit was not released in this way, there would be no rest, or the person would travel to the Other World with an incomplete soul.

If you happen to be visiting the Cliff Dwellings in the late fall when the weather is just beginning to grow damp and cold, the weather may help you realize what a difficult life these people led. The rooms in the dwellings are small and would be crowded if more than three or four people were to sit down together. During cold seasons this would be a good way to share body heat. The people who lived here are thought to have worn simple cotton garments, animal skins and some type of cape woven with strips of rabbit skin. There is also the suggestion that feathers were woven into the garments. It is not known if this was for warmth or ceremonial purposes. The bottom line is that these people did not have the kind of woolly protective clothes that are available today. Wintertime temperatures in this area are often below zero. Think about that as you zip up your down jacket.

The people left this area for reasons that are not entirely clear. Most likely they were unable to continue raising

*The Sun Spear — appears on the stone mural every year at the summer equinox. Constructed by the Anasazi Indians, this solstice marker was discovered in southwestern New Mexico by the photographer.*

enough food because of drought conditions. Or they may have felt the pressure of another more dominate group moving into the area. Whatever it was, they left their villages tucked under the cliffs and effectively disappeared leaving no forwarding address for today's archeologists. I am impressed when I look about at these remnants of past lives and remember that they were PEOPLE and they were HERE. I am a person and I am here, too. We have a connection in these old ruins, in this location. It is tenuous, but it is our shared humanity.

## The Copper Domain

From the Cliff Dwellings, you can travel down Highway 15 to Silver City and then drive around the loop seeing

Tyrone, Central, Bayard, Santa Rita, and the open pit mine belonging to Kennecott-Mitsubishi. If you didn't go to the Cliff Dwellings, but are still at the San Lorenzo junction and want to take the tour of the mining country, then stay on Highway 90.

You are entering the domain of the copper kings. It is not so much that Kennecott-Mitsubishi, Anaconda, and Phelps-Dodge own so much land in this part of New Mexico, but rather that the local economy and local lives have been so thoroughly intertwined with the copper industry for so long.

## The Santa Rita Pit

The road to Santa Rita will very quickly take you to the Santa Rita Pit. This, at one time, was the largest open pit copper mine on the planet. It is a gigantic hole in the earth. The Kennecott-Mitsubishi people have thoughtfully provided you a rest stop here so you can stop and look into this wonder. (The rest stop is also here so that the K-M company does not lose people who want to wander into the pit.) There is a recorded message available by the picnic tables so you can hear all kinds of statistics about how many trucks and how many men and how many tons. The statistics are almost meaningless because your attention may well be riveted on this pit, this enormous hole. The size of it is simply mind-boggling. It is beyond human proportion. As you look at it and wonder at it, you may want to remember that Kennecott did not dig this hole for any other reason that profit. No matter how many tons of copper were secured, no matter how many vital uses it has and what conveniences it brings to our lives, Kennecott profitted from every shovelful.

Leaving the pit, the road will take you through the small town of Santa Rita, on to Central on Highway 180 and down in to Bayard and Hurley.

## Salt of the Earth

This is the area where some of the most dramatic history involving unions, miners and film making in the United States took place. Essentially the recent history of this part of New Mexico is the basic story of the struggle between big company management and labor. The workers seek more safety, more wages — and the management seeks to protect its costs. Sometimes the struggles are justified one way and sometimes another.

In the mid nineteen-fifties the struggle between management and labor made union history. The miners, mostly Chicanos, led by an organizer for the United Mine Workers named Jenks, struck the mines at Hurley for better safety and living conditions. They wanted a buddy system in the mines for safety. Among the living conditions they wanted basic utilities in the company housing. Keep in mind that this was not the nineteenth century. This was the nineteen-fifties where everyone already was supposed to have a chicken in their pot and a car in their garage. In the prosperous fifties, these people merely wanted running water, electricity, and safe working conditions.

There followed a long strike, decorated with ugly tactics of harassment and violence by the management, and suffering by the union members. The Brotherhood of Trades, in the state of New Mexico sent food and supplies regularly to Hurley. The auxillary units of the unions collected clothes for the families out of work. It was a long and bitter strike.

At one point, the copper company obtained a court order making it illegal for the miners to maintain their picket line. Here history was made. The wives of the miners took their children and replaced their husbands on the picket line. This was a courageous move on the part of the women who were not liberated, well-educated members of the National Organization for Women. These women were housewives and mothers from a very traditional culture.

These brave ladies wanted to be sure that their men would come home from work every day. They wanted their children to grow up in safe and clean homes. They were led by the quiet wife of the union president. The copper company was outraged when it realized how it had been thwarted by mere women and they sent the sheriff to stop the women's activities. The ladies refused to leave the picket line and forced the sheriff to arrest them and take them to jail — babies and all. In the jail, chaos reigned. The jailors had to keep the ladies separated from the common criminals. The babies cried, they needed bottles and formulas. The ladies demanded proper food. The authorities were not prepared to deal with women and children. The press came. In the end, the ladies were released.

In the context of the times, all of this can only be described as outrageous. The strike was finally settled. Living conditions were improved, some safety measures were set in place. But the lives of the people were changed by the parts they had played. Men who had been breadwinners and heads of families had seen their wives act with courage and self-determination. Women had experienced the problem of dealing with power in the world outside of the home. There was triumph but there was confusion. The racial problems of Chicanos and Anglos had been dragged out into the open and sometimes had defeated the efforts of the people involved.

To intensify the stream of events, the United Mine Workers decided to make an accurate film of what had happened. The movie was called *"Salt of the Earth."* They felt they could add nothing dramatic since the events as they happened were almost larger than life. Everyone was asked to portray themselves. Actors were hired only for those roles where the actual participants declined to take part. The leading female actress of Mexico was hired to portray the wife of the union president.

The history of the film is almost as compelling as the history of the strike. First of all, it was a very well made movie. It was exciting, dramatic and it was true. Second of all, it so clearly showed the necessity and the good that could come from union organization that it immediately was seen as a threat to the members of the big business community. It was banned in many places, and the film makers could get no distribution. The leading lady was deported to Mexico where she was prevented from ever working in the film industry again. Technicians who worked on the film were black-balled and accused of communistic leanings. The film became a cult film that was shown at union halls and art theatres.

Jenks returned to school and got a doctorate. He is a tenured professor at Berkeley, and wears his blond hair in a pony tail hanging down his back. The union president is still living in the Silver City area with his wife, and is still working with the United Mine Workers. No one got rich or famous, or went to Hollywood. There is still some danger in mining. The management still provides company homes for the workers.

# TYRONE

Tyrone, which is 13 miles southwest of Silver City is the perfect example of the mining companies and their towns — and their power. This was a Phelps-Dodge town. Although it was named for a town in Ireland, when it fell under the auspices of Phelps-Dodge it was rebuilt as an exact replica of the city Leopold in Spain. It had a charming town square surrounded by public buildings and a hotel. The architecture was of Spanish-Moorish design with graceful arabesques and arches. It was a lovely place and it lasted until Phelps-Dodge decided to expand their operations and wanted to mine the area where Tyrone stood. Phelps-Dodge mined and the town was completely dismantled. Tyrone-Leopold no longer exists. The Tyrone you can find on the map today is a new and modern place that resembles nothing so much as a modern subdivision. Drive down the streets with names such as Malachite or Chryscola, and you see nice, ranch-style homes. Many of them are vacant because once again, copper prices are low and the entire Silver City area is in a depression with mining employment down.

## SILVER CITY

Silver City itself is a sprawling, western town. The university there is Western New Mexico University and it is a small, sound state institution. The history and folklore surrounding Silver City is dense. Almost anyone you meet will have a story or know someone who was an outlaw, a prospector or a lawman. Silver City is also one of the jumping-off places for trips into the Gila Wilderness, so there is even more to hear about that rugged back country.

Silver City does not look like a wild west town out of a movie. You will know you are not really in a big city when you wake up in the Holiday Inn and you hear coyotes calling.

## BAYARD

Just outside of Silver City on Highway 260 is Fort Bayard, or as it is usually called, just Bayard. This is the site of The Old Soldiers Home, as many New Mexicans call the hospital there. The place started out as an army garrison named for an army surgeon who researched the human digestive tract by watching what happened to food in the open gut of an injured soldier. (This was in the 1860's before patients knew they had rights.) The place eventually became a hospital for soldiers with tuberculosis, and other veterans. Finally the veterans hospital there was turned over to the state and it became the final stop for those with an incurable disease. It is still known as the old soldier's home, in spite of the changes that have taken place.

# HURLEY

Beyond Bayard, still on Highway 180 you will come to Hurley. As you drive south you will be able to see two white towers or smokestacks rising from the area of Hurley. These are the favorite targets of certain environmentalist groups who periodically sneak up to the top and unfurl banners accusing the smelters of polluting the air. No matter how you feel about pollution, you have to have a certain grudging respect for anyone who would attempt to shinny up those tall structures. Especially in the dark.

About eight miles past Hurley you will come to the place where Highway 61 meets Highway 180. If you turn left here you will be able to visit the City of Rocks State Park. If you decided not to visit the Gila Cliff Dwellings or the mining country around Silver City, you could have traveled to the City of Rocks by simply turning left at San Lorenzo. Highway 61 would have brought you to the City of Rocks after passing through San Juan, Dwyer and Mayfield. This is a gentle ride with glimpses of homes and ranches and fruit trees and cattle filling the time until you reach the City of Rocks turn-off or until you meet Highway 180.

As you come closer to Highway 180, the bucolic quality of the land begins to change and the dominate theme of southern New Mexico begins to take over. Once again you are treated to vastness. The golden grama grass sweeps all around and out to the very edges of the earth. The sky covers everything that the plains do not. There are vistas. There is land. There is space.

## The City of Rocks

The turn-off to the City of Rocks is well marked. It is about eight miles from the highway intersection. If you are approaching this spot during a weekend in the warm spring or summer, you should seriously consider going somewhere else. Warm weekends at the City of Rocks are crowded and noisy. Warm weekend nights at the City of Rocks are also crowded and noisy and they lock the rest rooms at five o'clock. Do not ruin this adventure for yourself. Go away and return some other time. It will be worth it, unless you are less of a wanderer and more of an extrovert.

The City of Rocks is a huge jumble of volcanic stones set in the middle of a vast and endless plain. As you explore it, walking among the monoliths and scrambling over boulders, you may begin to feel a definite sense of place or location. It is much like being in a town. You have traveled a distance and you have arrived. Nestled in among the stony monuments are campsites with picnic tables. Each seems to have been picked because it offered a special view or was next to a particularly spectacular rock.

*City of Rocks State Park — first view of the City of Rocks shows the stony city on the southwestern New Mexican plains.*

The special feeling of City of Rocks is that you are alone and in a private spot. A rare spot because the City of Rocks is also a botanical garden featuring some of the more unique desert plants. The wildlife is plentiful and if you have time, the ranger will tell you where to go to see owls, eagles, or other seasonal birds. Enhancing this special feeling is the fact that in the old part of the park there are no power lines or modern "comfort stations." The manmade buildings or safety features are all made out of the native stone and so blend into the landscape. The modern bathrooms and showers at the park entrance are always clean and neat and they seem appropriate in their setting.

The City of Rocks is surrounded with history and legend. The name itself is derived from the story told by grandmothers up and down the Mimbres Valley. It seems that at one time, in the times before Christ, there really had been a city on this wide and windy plain. Then, because the city was populated with people and people are heir to many faults, it was condemned by an angry god who was displeased by the behavior of the citizens. All of the inhabitants and all of the city were turned to stone. The curse of this god was to last forever unless a clever adventurer could find a hidden, magical cherry tree in the midst of the stone metropolis and bring the city back to life by chopping it down.

There are also legends of buried Spanish gold hidden among the towering rocks. The Spaniards were supposed to have packed copper from the Santa Rita area to Mexico and the pack trains were supposed to have camped here. Of course, one time the train was carrying gold and silver and the Spaniards were set upon by hostile Indians. The Spaniards buried the gold to keep it from the Indians but since all of the Spaniards were killed, their secret hiding spot perished with them. In the City of Rocks, you may find the crude pictures of crosses and swords scratched into the stones and attributed to those early Spanish adventurers. (Do not start digging for this gold. It is against the law to destroy state property and the state sees digging as destruction.)

Along with the pictures left by the Spanish, you will be able to see more rock pictures left by the Indians before the Spanish visited their land. The meaning of these pictures cannot be explained. It is a thought provoking experience to look at them and wonder about the person who made them, and what was on his mind while he laboriously engraved the rock.

The City of Rocks with its rare beauty and blend of man and nature is the perfect antidote to **too many people and too much world.** It is a retreat and an opportunity to savor the quiet; a pleasant time-out after the immediate history of the copper mines and the strident problems of Hurley's smokestacks and Santa Rita's giant pit.

If you want to participate more fully in nature, you may visit the hot springs next door, to the south of the entrance of the City of Rocks. A natural hot springs bubbles up out of the ground here, and there are a few primitive facilities. This is another spot to avoid on the weekends. You will get maximum pleasure and privacy here if you can come during the week and during the day. The land that the hot springs is on actually belongs to one of the copper companies. This company gave the hot springs to the state of New Mexico for the handicapped citizens. Unfortunately, the state lacked the money to develop such a facility, so the hot springs is open to the wanderer and other visitors.

When you finally tire of the traffic of squirrels and crowds of butterflies, it is time to wander on. Leave the City of Rocks, turn right at the exit and take Highway 61 to Highway 180. Turn left here and head for Deming, which is close to twenty-seven miles away. This stretch of Highway 180 may be the straightest road in the state. When you see it on a map, you know some highway engineer laid a straight-edge down, whipped out a line with his pencil and declared, "Let's build a road!" And they did.

# VII

# Deming to Columbus

# DEMING

Deming is a modest, small and sprawly town. The people are friendly and it is usually warm. In fact, it is sometimes referred to as *"the Riviera of New Mexico."* This is a gentle joke because although Deming is warm and pleasant, it has nothing to attract the chic or trendy. Unless the chic or trendy like ducks. Deming is home to the richest duck race in the world. It is probably the ONLY duck race in the world, but that doesn't bother anyone. In fact, it means the duck trainers have an entire uninterrupted year to train their racers. Ducks are trained to race down a track covered with chicken wire. Their trainers may perch on top of the wire, but it is forbidden to feed your duck green chile to make him run faster. While all of this sounds silly, it is silly to the tune of thousands of dollars per race.

*Treasures of the earth are displayed on every table at the Annual Rock Hound Round-up in Deming, New Mexico.*

There is also a Duck Queen contest for the ladies, and another contest for the best dressed duck. The last is for ducks who are dressed in little clothes by their owners. While all of this is going on, the population of Deming is doubled and everyone goes a little crazy. This is definitely not the same kind of fiesta as the one at La Joya or Hillsboro, but if you are in Deming in the late summer you should see how much fun adults can have with ducks and money.

In the early spring, usually in March, Deming is also the site of another international gathering. This is the Annual Rockhound Roundup, and people who like rocks or gems or minerals come from all over the country, as well as Canada and Mexico, to look at each other's rocks, buy, sell and trade. The manufacturers of tumbling machines, diamond saws and rock polishing equipment also send representatives to this meeting. Here you may buy Mexican fire opals, Canadian amethyst, Wyoming jade, as well as a blinding assortment of agates, turquoise, and minerals of all kinds. There will also be jewelry containing these stones. The quality of these objects, like the prices, range from just awful to simply amazing. And if you tire of looking at other people's handiwork, you can sign up for a field trip, and for a small fee you will be taken to a mineral field and be taught to look for your own minerals. The Deming area has a wide collection of agates, geodes and other fine rocks, so this is always an interesting experience.

## Rockhound State Park

Just a few miles south of Deming is Rockhound State Park where you are allowed to hunt for rocks on state land. You may keep whatever you find, but since the park has been open for many years, you must hike into the more distant areas of the park to find anything of value.

You may also camp out at Rockhound State Park. Showers and restrooms are available and there are covered picnic tables at each campsite.

If you are tired of camping out, you might stay in Deming. There are several new, modern, and clean hotels with famous names in Deming, and they will be exactly what you might expect and will cost much the same as their counterparts across the country. If, however, what you want is a clean place to sleep and shower, and you can forego the name brand inns, you should try the Bel Shore. The Bel Shore has no interior decoration worthy of the name but since you are sleeping, not looking, it doesn't matter. They seem to have endless supplies of hot water. The prices are more than reasonable, and everything is extremely neat and clean. The people who run the Bel Shore are also very amiable. This is a wanderers haven.

Deming is also the home of a well known psychic named Gilbert Holloway. If you are in need of this kind of assistance, you want to try and find this man. He frequently appears on radio talk shows.

## Deming to Columbus

Leave Deming by going south on Highway 11. As you travel away from Deming you will see the famous Deming Ranchettes. Deming Ranchettes were advertised for years in small black and white ads in the backs of small magazines. The ads promised wide open spaces and sun in the west, and that is exactly what the buyers got. The land was also dry and sandy, and the water was hundreds of feet down. But as you drive along you will see that several buyers of the Deming Ranchettes did build on the land and there are homes with green lawns and shrubs. There are still Deming Ranchettes for sale today and the prices are still low. You still get sunshine, land and sun.

The rugged and formidable Florida Mountains will be on your left or east as you cruise down the highway. In the distance on your right and slightly west, you will be able to see the Tres Hermanas Mountains. The *Three Sisters Mountains* are somewhat confusing because it will look like there are five mountains. Apparently, the two smaller ones, like little sisters all over the world, are to be ignored.

As you come to the occasional house, there will be large groves of trees by each one. The trees do not surround the houses but instead are growing around the tanks or the large manmade reservoirs that have been scraped into the desert.

## SUNSHINE

Halfway to Columbus you will pass a small hamlet called Sunshine. There is a store, a school, and a post office with a filling station. It has not been extensively explored by the author. Here's your perfect wanderer's chance.

After Sunshine, continue on down the highway. Just before you get to Columbus, you will see on the left side of the road, a long string of buildings or store fronts built in various styles. At one time there was some talk of legalizing gambling in this part of the country, and someone went to work to create an airfield-tourist attraction-casino. The legalization bill never made it through the state legislature and so the buildings remain in waiting. Once the owners tried to promote a festival called a Chicken Fly, where hens were dropped from the control tower to see whose could fly the farthest, but this activity never caught on like the duck races did.

# COLUMBUS

Columbus is home to approximately 500 people. It is a small place and it is quiet. There is a town hall for the matters of city government, a gas station, a post office, a grocery and variety store with video games, and a very small short-order restaurant-doughnut shop. There is also a bar, dark and cool, and a few second-hand shops. Ed Beck, one of the town's most energetic supporters, has a real estate office. There is also a small town library that is staffed by volunteers and has a wide selection of books, most of them donated. There is an elementary school and a laundromat. There is a small but efficient bank.

At first glance all of this is not immediately apparent. Columbus is spread out and you may feel that you have driven into a small and dusty spot that is the middle of nowhere. But it is not. Columbus is just not flashy. It has a sturdy volunteer fire department, two museums, several churches, a motel, and it is the home of Pancho Villa State Park.

A very attractive thing about Columbus is that everything is within walking distance except the laundromat. The laundromat is fairly close to the Mexican border (about 3 miles from the center of town) and that becomes something of a trek when you are toting dirty clothes, detergent and extra quarters. (Incidentally, the newest Mexican pesos are exactly the same weight and size as U.S. quarters, so do not feel affronted if someone in the laundromat wants to know what exactly you are putting in the coin slots.)

## Columbus and Pancho Villa

Columbus is very relaxed, very calm, and there are many things to do and see here. It is usually warm, the wind usually stirs a bit and in the summer it is very hot.

Columbus is also the only spot in the continental United States ever to have been invaded by an enemy from a foreign country since the U.S. won the war for Independence. On March 9, 1916, Pancho Villa and his soldiers raided Columbus, New Mexico, and after terrorizing the town, setting fires and killing some of the citizens, these firey revolutionaries were chased back to Mexico. Soldiers of the United States Army who were stationed at Camp Furlong, in the town of Columbus, pursued and killed many of the Mexican attackers.

This part of history is very much a part of reality here in Columbus. Some of the people living in Columbus today were present during Villa's raid. Some of the buildings standing in the town were those that escaped Villa's fires.

The first time I visited Columbus I stood in awe before buildings that were pockmarked with bullets from the raid. Not only is the invasion real to the citizens of Columbus, it became real to me on that day. I could imagine the streets filled with galloping horses, the air filled with smoke from the burning buildings, and the fear of death all around. It somehow was more immediate than any news broadcast on television, or any radio announcement. The landscapes, the way of life, and this part of New Mexico has not been dramatically changed since that day in 1916. Columbus grew smaller and now there are fewer buildings, fewer people, and fewer services, but the place remains the same.

The mystery behind Villa's raid also remains. At the time, the raid was a surprise and no one really knew why Pancho Villa picked Columbus and what he hoped to accomplish.

Harris, in his book on Pancho Villa, claims that Villa raided Columbus because he had a personal debt to settle with the merchant Sam Ravel, who was said to have cheated the revolutionary leader. Rakocy, in the book *"Villa Raids Columbus, New Mexico"* discusses other theories about deals that Villa might have made with the government of Germany or the government of the United States.

The reading is fascinating but it does not have the intensity of the old man who told me that Pancho Villa and his men raided Columbus to steal 18 sacks of gold from the Southern Pacific Railway. They buried it in the desert when the U.S. army pursued them. The hiding place of the gold was then concealed by the rumor that there were men buried in the ground at that site, not sacks of gold. And like all buried treasure stories, the exact site has been lost, and the gold is still waiting. But the desire to have the gold was alive in the old man's eyes.

Villa's raid did have several effects on the U.S. army. It occurred at a time when technology was just catching up to warfare. When U.S. troops under Black Jack Pershing were transferred to Camp Furlong to hunt down and capture Villa, they were aided by high tech. This was to become the first time that airplanes were used by the United States in pursuit of the enemy. The fledgling Army Air Corp had two cloth-covered biplanes to scout for Villa. The old airstrip is still marked out west of Columbus and it is a fine place to go and look for old army buttons and lost insignia.

This was also the first time that the automobile was to become a planned part of the action and the first grease racks ever constructed on a military installation were built at Camp Furlong. The grease racks are still standing in Pancho Villa State Park, which was built around this old abandoned army post. The supply trucks were driven onto the grease racks and the mechanics crawled beneath them to do the maintenance work.

There must have been a great deal of maintenance to do. The land around Columbus and Pancho Villa State Park is rugged and thorny. The land that Villa retreated to was also inhospitable. Villa was a skilled guerilla fighter and he led Pershing and his men through some of the roughest terrain in Mexico. The U.S. army moved in a column as it always had, accompanied by supply trucks and equipment wagons. Villa moved through the country as he always had, depending on the land and the people to supply his needs. Pershing never caught up with the two gun revolutionary. It was bound to be one of the wildest chase scenes in history.

Fortunately, or unfortunately, the demands of World War I called the troops away from New Mexico and the Villistas and on to Germany. Some people speculated that the United States government used the raid on Columbus as an excuse to get soldiers into the field and conditioned for the battles in Europe. Others say that it was a lucky break that World War I allowed the U.S. a graceful excuse to quit the search for Villa. Whatever point of view is taken, there is no denying that the chapter of history featuring Pershing and Villa is as dramatic, mysterious and colorful as any lie that could be invented.

## Dave's Picture of Pancho Villa _____

Dave's grandfather grew up in Texas, an orphan. He graduated from college at a time when it was popular to finish when you were about seventeen. His guardian then sent him to medical school in Mexico City. According to Dave, at that time it was easy for a gringo with money to get into medical school and pass. After medical school, Dave's grandfather moved to Silver City. There he worked with the poorer people and those who wouldn't go to doctors. He treated his patients with herbs to help them over the stomachache, backache, or headache. During this time he occasionally treated Pancho Villa's men for their small aches and pains.

He invested in mining operations and a brewery in Mexico and went there regularly on business trips.

*left to right, front row seated: 1-criada, 2-blank, 3- Pancho Villa, 4-Mrs. Martinez, 4-Senor Martinez, 5-Carl Hoguelin of the Brewery.*
*back row, right to left: 6-Senor Martinez half brother, 8-Senor Joaquin Baurget, a French merchant, 10-Villa's secretary and aide, 11-Villa's first lieutenant.*
*As far as known this photograph has not been published before.*

This photograph was found among Dave's grandfather's things when he died. His widow burned all of his records and travel diaries, but kept the picture. The photograph was probably taken by a Mexican photographer and given to Dave's grandfather by the brewery owner, who is shown seated on the far right in the front row. The handwriting on the bottom of the photograph identifies Pancho Villa among the other people in the picture. Written on the back is the following statement: "July 29, 1920 — at Sabinosa Coahicila Mexico — upon the occasion of Pancho Villa's visit with 500 soldiers. He was in charge there for one week, the National Government eventually capitulated and gave him a big ranch in the state of Sinola. This picture was taken at the house of Senor Martinez, a prominent Spanish merchant — after Pancho had invited himself and staff for *'dinner'*."

On the bottom of the picture someone has written names to match the numbers that were also handwritten on the photograph. Not everyone is identified and some only cryptically. For example number 1 is *'criada'* which is the Spanish word for maid. Both Senor and Mrs. Martinez are identified by a number 4.

## The Columbus Historical Society Museum ____

Visit the museum in the old railroad station. This is another museum by the people - for the people. Established by the volunteers of the Columbus Historical Society, this museum not only has a wonderful collection of pictures and newspapers about the epic of Columbus and the Villa raid, it also has a great variety of artifacts pertaining to everyday life in New Mexico before and at the time of the raid. This is a wonderful museum and it takes time to see everything. A very exciting aspect of visiting this museum is the fact that the museum volunteer on duty may have been the person who donated some of the artifacts to the museum. They may also be one of the survivors of the raid. The picture on the wall, or the dress on display may have been a family treasure. Ask about the displays and you may get a history lesson from someone who was there.

## The Old Customs House_____

Across the street from the railroad station is the old Customs House. This was in use until the early fifties when the U.S. Customs Service and Immigration moved down the road to its present location right on the border. Now it is the domain of the park service and it, too, has a small display on the Villa raid. It presents a film, recently made, that shows the survivors of Villa's raid relating where they were and how they saw the raid. It is a shock to see these elderly people talking about Villa and the fear and damage that he caused to their families, their neighbors, and their home town. If nothing else in Columbus will make Pancho Villa's raid real to you, this film will. The film is shown twice daily and the hours are posted on the door of the Customs House. Across the street from the Customs House is the entrance to Pancho Villa State Park.

## Pancho Villa State Park

Pancho Villa State Park was the site of the army camp, Camp Furlong. Remnants of the army buildings remain, and there are signs explaining what each building was. When the park was established and given the name of Pancho Villa, there was some controversy over this. Some people felt it was inappropriate to name a state park after an enemy of the United States, especially a man who had murdered American citizens. Others felt that Villa had put Columbus on the map and he should be honored for that. After a time, the controversy died down and the name remained.

Pancho Villa State Park is also a carefully tended botanical garden. There are large and lush specimens of ocotillo, yucca, prickly pear, palo verde, century plants and chamisa, to name a few. The plants are artistically arranged among the camp sites and picnic areas, and besides beauty, they provide effective screens to make each camp site isolated from the others. In the fall the prickly pear can be in full fruit. Check with the park management about gathering and eating some of this cactus fruit. It is tasty, but great care must be taken with the spines.

For the bird watcher, this park is a veritable paradise. During early March I once spotted 14 different birds within an hour. They were snow geese, sandhill cranes, robins, sparrows, juncoes, Gambel's quail, roadrunners, flickers, shrike, kildeer, prarie falcon, mourning doves, crows, and a Pyrruhloxia finch. The snow geese were particularly thrilling as they flew across the face of the moon in the early morning light.

Early morning and late evening are enhanced by the carillon in the local Catholic Church. At these times a lovely and delicate melody calls the people to their prayers and the notes float over the park.

The park also has practical features. There are showers and restrooms that are open all night. There are two playgrounds equipped with swings and slides and merry-go-rounds for the children. There is a dump station for recreational vehicles and extra large picnic areas to accommodate large groups. The personnel at Pancho Villa are all pleasant and well informed about their park. They will appear in the mornings to collect the camping fee and will be able to answer any question you might have.

## The Old Army Dump

Another advantage to Pancho Villa Park is its close proximity to the old army dump. About a quarter of a mile behind Pancho Villa Park, across a field, is the old army dump. If the field is not planted, you may walk across it. If it is in use, there is a road that runs parallel to the highway, that you may walk. The dump has been hunted by hundreds of people since the army left Columbus. This doesn't seem to matter. You can still find army buttons, coins, harness insignia, and buckles. There are old bottles and battery cores. Crockery from the mess halls and ink pots from the supply rooms can also be picked up. You don't need metal detectors to find these treasures. After a rain or wind, these objects are exposed on the surface for the modern day amateur archeologist to pick up. Nobody cares what you pick up, nobody will mind if you dig a deep pit because you have a hunch that a wonderful find is just below the surface. The dump is a grimy place because of sand and dirt, and dump hunting should be done in casual clothes, preferably old ones. It is a great place to get a sun tan as you hunt. Many of the found things will be tarnished and encrusted with dirt. A little soap and water will do much to restore your finds. Brasso is always good on the insignia, or a little vinegar and water.

The most exciting discovery I made in the dump was a coin from the Phillipines dated before Villa's raid. I marveled how such a coin could have traveled around the world and come to my hand in Columbus, New Mexico. Then I read that the military unit that was stationed at Camp Furlong during Villa's raid had been in the Phillipine Islands before being transferred to New Mexico. I often wonder if I had picked up some soldier's good-luck piece, and how he fared during the pursuit of Pancho Villa.

# PALOMAS, MEXICO

If you tire of the peace and history of Columbus, travel three miles south and you may enter Mexico. The town across the frontier is Palomas and you are in a foreign country. Take your I.D. with you. Leave your car in the parking lot at the border. No one will stop you from driving across but should you have **any** kind of traffic accident, the ensuing red tape, legal entanglements and possible time in a Mexican jail will make a summit conference in Geneva look like a Sunday School picnic.

The attractions of Palomas are 1) you are in a strange country, 2) it is picturesque, 3) liquor and some other items are very inexpensive. Do walk around this small town. The people are used to gringos and after a few blocks you will be convinced you are not at home. Two blocks down the main street and a turn to your right will bring you to the plaza and the church. In the spring and early summer you can sit in this public park and watch the world go by. The church is very photogenic and there will probably be a few children about whom you can talk to.

Besides the church and the business of the customs office, the main event in Palomas is Tilly. Tilly is a shrewd business woman who has been doing business in Palomas for years and years and years. Tilly looks like she is about forty, but she has always looked this way. She looked like this in the early fifties, she looked like this in the eighties. She is a friendly lady who speaks English and runs the larger bar-restaurant-liquor-curio-grocery store in Palomas. She can probably also advise you about anything else you might want to know about Palomas and Mexico in general. You will see Tilly's establishment on your left as you walk into town. The last time I was there, it was painted blue. Visit it last, before you leave, so you won't have to tote your purchases with you as you stroll.

It is hard to suggest what you should look for in Palomas. If you like wine, buy some Los Reyes Tinto Vino. If you like liqueurs, Mexico is famous for Kahlua, a coffee flavored one. You may also see an assortment of regular tourist stuff like embroidered shirts, serapes, dolls, pottery, and blue glass. Depending on the value of the peso, people on the U.S. side sometimes shop in Mexico for such staples as powdered milk or crackers because they can be cheaper. Bear in mind that these are products made in Mexico and they may not meet your expectations. Sometimes they are better, sometimes they are worse, ususlly they are merely different.

In the Palomas-Columbus area each adult may bring back one bottle or 750 milliliters of liquor apiece and not be obliged to pay any tax or duty on it. You may bring back more if you wish, but you must pay duty and tax on the extra bottles. To do this, you must stop at the Customs House on the U.S. side and declare what you have purchased. The customs agent then will figure out what you must pay for import duty as well as for state tax. The amounts are not very large, but this takes some time. The agents are very meticulous about doing it properly and they know what they are doing. This is an example of your tax money at work. The cost for extra liquor is usually only a few pennies and some extra time.

## Raid Day

On March ninth, every year, the people of Columbus and the Historical Society commemorate the day that Pancho Villa invaded the country. The event is known locally as *"Raid Day"* and it is a memorial for the people who lost their lives. Raid Day is a pure example of American small town

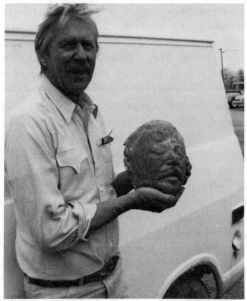

*Bill Rakocy, of the El Paso Museum of Art, holds Poncho Villa's death mask.*

celebration. I have attended this many times and each time was different, but each was enjoyable. Go to Raid Day if you are the kind of person who gets a lump in the throat when you see the flag raised while a junior high kid plays trumpet.

On Raid Day, the memorial celebration takes place on Coot's Hill in the Pancho Villa Park. This is the hill where the flag is flying. Everyone walks up the hill along the neatly marked paths between the cactus. The wind is usually blowing. There will be survivors from the raid, town government personnel, and members of the Historical Society. If it is on a school day, the elementary school might be present. There is usually a color guard from nearby Fort Bliss in El Paso. One time an old soldier from Bayard came, resplendent in his uniform complete with puttees. I don't know if Today's Army still issues puttees. The soldier also brought his trumpet and played "Taps" for his fallen comrades. He didn't come back the next year and a very young soldier played "Taps" on the old horn and wore the uniform. It didn't sound the same.

Miss New Mexico is invited to this pageant, and one time she did come and she read a proclamation from the governor. The governor is always invited. Sometimes he sends a representative, sometimes he doesn't. This can become a hot issue during an election year. A local minister says a prayer and the Veterans of Foreign Wars put the flag at half-mast. There is a guest speaker, and someone will lead the crowd in "My Country Tis of Thee." The whole thing lasts about twenty minutes but it is moving. Then everyone goes over to the Railway Station- Museum for lunch. One time the ladies of the Historical Society served lunch to everyone who attended the memorial. In a true display of Southwestern hospitality they served chicken salad sandwiches and homemade cake to their neighbors and tourists alike. There is sometimes a flea market conducted at the same time. Like all flea markets there is a treasure or a piece of junk at every table. After lunch the Park Service will show the film about the Raid. The whole day is an experience in nostalgia.

Check the notice boards by the doors to the restrooms in Pancho Villa State Park for other notices about Raid Day activities. One time Tilly offered a steak luncheon special on Raid Day and even had flamenco dancers from Juarez for entertainment. The whole thing was well worth the money.

To find out exact details for each years' Raid Day, call the Columbus Town Hall in early March or late February.

# VIII

# Columbus to Antelope Wells
### including
### Hachita
### The Big Hatchet Wildlife Refuge
### Antelope Wells

## Columbus to Hachita

Heading west from Pancho Villa State Park, you will be driving toward Hachita, New Mexico on Highway 9. You will be passing through more flat desert, covered with chaparral and mesquite. Chaparral, the thorny, bushy shrubs that cover the desert is the reason cowboys wear chaps or leather protectors over their legs. Chaps is a shortened form of the Spanish word *"chaparejos"* which is derived from the word for the vegetation.

Much of this wide and rugged land can be cultivated successfully if water is brought to it. From the road, one can see the concrete lined irrigation ditches designed to do just this.

About fourteen miles from the Pancho Villa State Park you will be able to see a commercial onion shed. Beyond it, in the distance to the south and in Mexico, is a large lake, Laguna de Guzman. Laguna de Guzman seems out of place in this desert and you might think it a mirage, except it doesn't move about and waver as mirages usually do.

The landscape is open and vast. The road is following the route of the old Southern Pacific Railroad. On the right is the old roadbed. If you stop on the side of the highway and get out and walk between the *"bob wire"* fence and the coal covered roadbed, you might find an old bottle that some long ago passenger threw from the train window. Or you might find an old railroad artifact like a bottle of Edison acid for putting in the batteries on the warning lights at the crossings. In this area I once came upon an old iron door about twelve by twelve inches. It was buried half way in the dirt and it was obviously some part of a train. The date stamped on the metal read 1908.

The paved highway eventually narrows, leaving you on a smaller dusty, two lane road. Enjoy the wide sky, the open space, and the mountains receding in grey shadows far away. Savor the clean air and hold all of this in memory for your next urban traffic snarl.

About forty-five miles from Pancho Villa State Park, on the right side of the road, you will be able to spot the old black water tower left from the days when the old Southern and Pacific Railroad stopped here. This is Hachita, New Mexico and it is on the left side of the road.

Hachita is derived from the Spanish word that means *"signal hill"* or *"little torch."* And the U.S. cavalry did have a heliograph system in these parts around the time that Hachita was established in the 1880's. However Hachita also gave rise to the English word for *"hatchet"* or *"small axe"* so take your pick of meanings. The two local mountain ranges are known as the Big Hatchet Mountains and the Little Hatchet Mountains.

Look to the north and you will be able to see the ruins of old Hachita. When Hachita was a mining town, it was grouped around the mine shaft on this hillside. You may still drive up to old Hachita and wander among the ruins of houses and peer into the dark mine entrances.

Drive around Hachita and you will be able to see a melange of old abandoned adobe buildings, new mobile homes, and neat traditional buildings. And satellite dishes. There is a gas station in Hachita, a post office, Freddy's General Store and Auto Parts, as well as a Baptist Church and a Catholic Church. Hachita has a population of under one hundred people and it is not growing too much at this time.

The Catholic Church, Saint Catherine of Siena, is one of the more unusual buildings in Hachita. Located on Highway 81, it is a white building with an arresting stone portico and bell tower. The stone work looks like it was added after the building was built, and indeed it was. The white structure used to be the school house when Hachita had a bigger population. The children now ride the bus to Animas, thirty miles away.

The school house was purchased by Daniel Suozzi, a retired business man who came west to live in the warm climate. A religious man, Suozzi converted the old school to a church and named it after his mother, Catherine. He heard that an elegant old church was being torn down in New York State, so he took a cattle truck to the East and returned to Hachita with furnishings for the new church. There are 800 pound brass bells, made in Spain hanging in the bell towers. Inside, there are old and artistic stations of the cross that were made in Germany. The church is a place of color and light. Great light fixtures of glass hang from the ceiling and a red carpet covers the aisle. A visitor leaves the impression that the church is a place of special importance to the members.

Dan Suozzi is a man bringing change to Hachita. He moved to the small town in the early seventies and bought a large ranch. He began to learn the cattle business as a second career in his sixties. He had a great deal of experience with the

out-of-doors from his years spent as a big game hunter in the
Americas and Africa. He had a great deal of business experience from his years spent in the automobile industry on
the east side of the United States. In Hachita he is working on
renewing the town. He is encouraging the formation of town
government, a volunteer fire and ambulance service, as well
as other city services. He encourages retirees to come and live
in the year round sunshine and offers them land for new
homes. Dan Suozzi sees progress in Hachita and from his
point of view it will be for the good.

*Saint Catherine of Siena Church — stands in Hatchita,
New Mexico, a statement about one man's determina-
tion and efforts.*

In his late seventies, Suozzi is a charming, approachable
man. He is a dynamo of energy and a force to be reckoned
with. He lives outside of Hachita in a refurbished adobe that
was once a two room house for nine people, and is now an
inviting and impressive home made from stone.

Leaving Hachita, going south on Highway 81 you will be on the road to Antelope Wells. This settlement on the U.S.-Mexican border is as far south as you can travel in New Mexico.

As you travel you will have the Big Hatchet peak on your left. It is 8444 feet high, and it is a brooding presence on the desert. The cool, grey-shadowed mountain peaks on the right gather in the New Mexico *"bootheel"* to form San Luis Pass.

Again you will be driving through land whose enormity stretches without boundary to the mountain peaks. It is land to make the heart soar and the mind ponder the word freedom. This is not a place for the timid, or the soul who craves white picket fences.

The bootheel of New Mexico is the home of wild critters and the equally rare working cowboy. Scan the horizons for that legendary man on the horse. He is still here, working the cattle in a changing industry.

## The Big Hatchet Wildlife Refuge

Thirteen miles out of Hachita is a narrow dirt road on the left and a sign that says Big Hatchet Wildlife Refuge. The wildlife is protected here and in the early spring you will be able to spot true ravens and kestrels.

The road is narrow and dirt, and it slowly twists and turns its way across the desert. Although you will pass a ranch house or two, you will see few other signs of people. In fact, once away from the houses, the absence of people and manmade marks is striking. There are a few fences here but there are no power lines. There are no telephone wires. The land is wide and windy and lonesome. It is difficult to tell how far you are from the Mexican border because of the way the road winds. Although you cannot get lost as long as you stay on the road, you may experience a touch of apprehension mixed with the pleasure of isolation. It would be POSSIBLE to get lost in this landscape. It is a feeling in your gut.

If you are equipped to camp out, this is a rare spot. Pick a spot off the road in case there is some wandering night traffic. The coyotes' singing is the only true noise. The silence and the buzz of silence fills the air. The sun goes down and without a moon there is only velvety black darkness. The nocturnal creatures will not appear for some time and you will be alone in the great silence. This is something to try.

*Vastness — twentieth century man's crowning achievement, the pick-up truck, is dwarfed by the landscape in the vastness of the Big Hatchet Wildlife Refuge.*

Something to experience. You may not like it at all. It may bring you satisfaction. Whatever your emotion, it will be transcendant; the sun will reappear in eight hours and your time in the dark and silence will be over. Retrace your steps to the main road.

Still heading south you will see a smelter on your right. It belongs to Mining and Mining Corporation of America. All the signs posted by the corporation invite you to keep your ass out of their domain. The language is pure legalese but the meaning is unmistakable. On your left you will see a tall spire of rock, a *"thumb"* reaching up from the Big Hatchet Mountain. Look closely at this impressive mountain, and near the top you will be able to make out a face with an exceptionally large, beaky nose and deep sunken eyes.

. The country is beautifully monotonous here. It is flat and covered with the fierce, thorny chaparral. This might not fit closely with the typical desert description of sand dunes and cactus, but it is desert never-the-less. There are cactus but no soft shifting dunes. The ground is bitter, hard and gravelly. As you drive by you may see the irrigation systems of the Western Pacific Land and Cattle Company. They too wish you away from their land with equally inhospitable signs.

Approximately thirty miles outside of Hachita, the pavement ends. The road is now dirt, but well maintained and driveable. On the right you will see a neat and trim white house. It seems an anachronism in this harsh land. The main vegetation has now changed from chaparral to yucca. It is a regular yucca bazaar and the scent of blooming white flowers is exquisite in May. Surely it must have been May when the first Spaniards saw the Yuccas and named them *"Candles of God."*

The next signpost will direct you to High Lonesome. It guides you to the left and all that is apparent is an extra large windmill. There is no doubt that this is a lonesome spot.

## ANTELOPE WELLS

One mile from the Mexican border is the settlement of Antelope Wells. It is a small and ragged collection of mobile homes, pay phones, and a cattle chute and holding pen. There is a great deal of cattle commerce back and forth across the Mexican border. There is also a Customs agent stationed here. Antelope Wells is a port of entry between the two countries. It is a lonely spot and at one time the bus ride from Antelope Wells to the school at Hachita was considered to be the longest school bus ride in the United States. It was forty-six miles each way.

Although the road takes you to Antelope Wells, you may not be able to enter. When diplomatic relationships between the United States and Mexico are tense, the Customs agent will invite you to leave. During these times, the United States considers all tourists as liabilities and they do not want to be responsible for you. If there is going to be a border incident, the federal government would prefer it only involve their employees. Naturally, times like these make the Customs agents edgy. Take this, as well as current events, into consideration when you travel to Antelope Wells.

The map of New Mexico shows that you may pass through Antelope Wells and go on to Cloverdale, where Highway 338 will take you to Animas. Be aware that the twenty-one mile stretch between Antelope Wells and Cloverdale can be closed because of weather or border problems. The customs agent will let you know how far you can travel.

# Roads End

The wanderer's road ends at Antelope Wells. I invite you to return home as best you can, going by roads you choose and looking for adventure and pleasure as you will.

If you make plans to travel into other parts of the state you might want to look for the other Wanderer's Guides for the northwest, northeast, and southeast quadrants of New Mexico. There is also a special edition for the area containing the Gila Wilderness. ¡Buen Viaje!

# INDEX

# ORDER FORM

To order more copies of the Wanderer's Guide, complete the form below and mail it to:

**D. NAKII ENTERPRISES**
**P.O. Box 7639**
**Albuquerque, New Mexico 87194**

$6.95 per copy plus $1.50 postage and handling

Discounts available for large orders. Send inquiries to address above. Please send check or money order. Continental USA only.

Name _____

Address _____

City_____    State_____    Zip_____

Number of copies_____    Amount enclosed _____

Postage & Handling _____

Total _____